**ACTIVITY AND PLAY
OF CHILDREN**

PRENTICE-HALL
INTERNATIONAL
RESEARCH MONOGRAPH SERIES
IN PHYSICAL EDUCATION

H. Harrison Clarke, Chairman of the Editorial Board

Activity and Play
of Children

M. J. ELLIS
Dalhousie University

G. J. L. SCHOLTZ
Potchefstroom University for Christian Higher Education

Prentice-Hall, Inc.
Englewood Cliffs, New Jersey   07632

Library of Congress Cataloging in Publication Data

ELLIS, MICHAEL J.   (date).
    Activity and play of children.

    Bibliography: p. 132
    Includes index.
    1. Play.   2. Child psychotherapy.   I. Scholtz,
G. J. L., joint author.   II. Title.
BF717.E42   155.4'12   77-24286
ISBN 0-13-003574-2

© 1978 by Prentice-Hall, Inc., *Englewood Cliffs, N.J.   07632*

Printed in the United States of America

10   9   8   7   6   5   4   3   2   1

PRENTICE-HALL INTERNATIONAL, INC., *London*
PRENTICE-HALL OF AUSTRALIA PTY. LIMITED, *Sydney*
PRENTICE-HALL OF CANADA, LTD., *Toronto*
PRENTICE-HALL OF INDIA PRIVATE LIMITED, *New Delhi*
PRENTICE-HALL OF JAPAN, INC., *Tokyo*
PRENTICE-HALL OF SOUTHEAST ASIA PTE. LTD., *Singapore*
WHITEHALL BOOKS LIMITED, *Wellington, New Zealand*

*This monograph is dedicated to all the children who played for us,
and to all those named below who conducted the research:*

A. Balter	S. Haines	K. Newell
L. Barnett	B. Haynes	R. Ramsden
D. Bishop	R. Herron	R. Reynolds
A. Blair	J. Hughes	A. Rittenhouse
R. Bohrer	C. Jeanrenaud	G. Roberts
B. Cooke	E. Kamon	P. Rzepka
B. Costa	D. Kennedy	J. Samson
T. Craig	R. Korb	T. Scanlan
K. DeOreo	Y. Lambert	P. Schmitz
B. Dunn	D. Landers	G. Scholtz
J. Duthie	L. Lanto	D. Smith
M. Ellis	J. Levy	R. Sprague
G. Franklin	A. Linford	S. Tewes
M. Frobish	M. Linford	M. Wade
R. Geeseman	M. McDonald	I. Williams
P. Graham	K. McQuarrie	P. Witt
A. Gramza	R. Martens	L. Wuellner
L. Grover	B. Nixon	

Contents

Preface

This monograph integrates and summarizes the research on and theorizing about play behavior conducted by members of the Motor Performance and Play Research Laboratory, Children's Research Center, University of Illinois, from 1966 through 1973. In the work of the laboratory, as in any science, there is an intimate integration between the current thinking and the thinking that has gone before. While the main emphasis in this treatment is placed on the work conducted in this laboratory, the debt to others is acknowledged in the best way possible. Wherever the inclusion of another scientist's work or thinking adds to the development or a coherent view of play itself, then it has been incorporated.

Play research is still in its infancy. Play and play behavior, however, have been the subject of conjecture and theorizing for many centuries. The history of the notions concerning play reaches far back into the Greek civilizations and probably beyond. However, it wasn't until quite recently that concern for play has moved beyond the speculative. Now it is not enough to derive neat semantic or conceptual schemes for separating the "trivial" material of play from the "crucial" activities of work.

The literature of the Western World shows that there have been two major bursts of research activity on play. The first, which was mainly empirical in nature, flourished during the 1920's and 1930's and was largely concerned with descriptive reports of the overt play behavior of children together with catalogs of their activities. There were occasional experiments, but these were seriously hampered by the lack of scientifically based theory as well as a lack of inferential statistical procedures for testing the problems of concern. This early burst of enthusiasm was presumably deflected by the wars in Europe and Asia that occurred during the 1940's and 1950's, and it wasn't until after the post-Sputnik scare in America that play behavior once again came to be seen as a worthy area of scientific endeavor.

The second stage started toward the end of the 1950's and continues to the present. This second upwelling of interest in research on play behavior derived from an increasing concern for enriching and managing the lives of young children. This concern was derived quite simply from an increasing acceptance of the impact of the early environment on development and competence. In general, the work in this stage has been analytical and experimental. There has been a concern with the testing of hypotheses and the developing of theoretical systems which would enable an individual, whether he be a scientist or a practicing professional, to make general statements and predictions about play behavior. It has been made possible by the burgeoning maturity of the experimental and statistical methods available in the behavior sciences. To these developments could be added the fact that the federal government was heavily committed to the support of science and indirectly some of those resources facilitated research on children's play.

The coming together of these important influences encouraged play research. However, it would be a mistake to give the impression that suddenly many researchers decided to study play behavior. The amount of research done on play was, and still is, extremely limited, but the 1960's saw the beginning of several research efforts. One of those research efforts was mounted at the *Motor Performance and Play Research Laboratory* in the Children's Research Center of the University of Illinois. That laboratory was established in one of the centers established by the federal government to promote interdisciplinary research on questions of social concern.

The children's Research Center (CRC) at the University of Illinois was established to study learning and emotional disorders. One of the research teams established in that center was given the mandate to study the processes whereby children and exceptional children acquire motor skills and to study their behavior during those periods of time during their day that the children were engaged in informal activities. The first part of the mandate was in accord with the notion that the more retarded a child, the more prized become the available motor skills. This approach was concerned with the processes involved in the acquisition of such prized skills and rapidly extended itself to include the acquisition of skill in general.

The other mandate grew directly from an interactionist view of development. It was obvious that children were born into the world with genetically determined limits, and yet the realization of those limits was influenced dramatically by their interaction with the environment. It was recognized that at this time manipulating the genetic materials was impossible. For the developmental and caring professions to produce effects on their children, they were left with environmental manipulation. One aspect of those environmental interactions involved the child in the informal or play setting. Since often about half a child's waking time was spent in informal activity, the impact of the informal environment was clearly an area of major importance. For these reasons the play research laboratory was established.

The play research laboratory, a constituent lab of the Motor Performance and Play Research Laboratory was established in 1966. The main laboratory itself was, in fact, no more than just a room. That room, 21 × 30, was the space in which a very large number of experiments was conducted by a group of people brought together to study the informal behavior of children. That group of people, members of the Motor Performance and Play Research Laboratory, and the students that have clustered around then, operated on a tiny budget of perhaps less than $50,000 to $60,000 per year and has been one of the few settings in which the scientific study of play behavior has been actively conducted.

The research conducted since 1966 has followed on several themes; for example some members were studying activity patterns, others were studying stereotyped behavior, and yet others were concerned with preference for objects and peers. The research has, in general, been published in a great variety of scholarly journals. There are also a significant number of internal reports that have something to say yet are not individually important enough to satisfy the peer review process. Although these were conducted in parallel, it became obvious toward the end that there was a common theoretical underpinning to this research, but the relationships among themes are not available to those outside the laboratory.

It is the purpose of this monograph to integrate the findings and thinking that were directed at play behavior in the Motor Performance and Play Research Laboratory. It is hoped that the monograph shows that, collectively, the papers and reports sum to a far more cohesive and important body of work as a whole than when the separate elements are left to stand alone.

By 1973, seven years after the first project, research in the laboratory had come to a natural watershed in that it began to change in character. New research thrusts had moved from the large naturalistic settings and began to emphasize controlled laboratory studies. This move resulted from the need to test the more specific theories that were derived from the earlier studies. The work presented here stops at that point.

This monograph has had the benefits of hindsight in its organization. The contents are presented in their best light. The ideas are presented linearly in an arrangement that leads most directly and simply to what seems to be an appropriate conclusion. The organization of theory is laid out in the simplest possible form. The impression to be gained, then, is one of the laboratory operating in an exceptionally orderly fashion. This, of course, will reinforce the view that science is a magic intellectual activity that leads with parsimony to understanding. However, the laboratory had worked during those seven years in a ferment of confusion as the creative process of problem solving was applied to some of the intriguing questions about a child's play behavior. This report excludes the muddled thinking and the confusions that characterize any human activity, let alone years of research.

The research process itself looks like the definitions of play behavior. If play is in fact exploration, investigation, and manipulation of events, objects and ideas in the environment, then so has been this research program. Therefore, *caveat emptor*. This monograph was ordered into a theoretically concise and cohesive whole *after the fact*. However, its potential cohesion and theoretical unification was clearly understood by 1969. In fact, during that year several important discussions on the nature of play took place and eventually stimulated one of the authors to write a book entitled *Why People Play*, which had two chapters devoted to an explanation for play that sustained much of the research conducted between 1969 and the end of 1973.

With these cautions, then, this monograph can be read. It contains a mixture of six chapters, some are essays and some are reviews of research. Each chapter follows a clearly defined theme, thus again contributing to the notion that we were an orderly group. However, it was the authors of this monograph who have disentangled and ordered the material. In the real life of the laboratory many experiments bearing sometimes on more than one different idea were undertaken at the same time.

The monograph begins with a brief introduction to the problem and the methods brought to bear on it. The first chapter, *Introduction and Methods*, is a story of how and why the methods used in the rest of the research were developed. This chapter is followed by a chapter that gives a *Theoretical Overview* of the theoretical bases of the research presented. However, since much of the theory was originally presented in Chapters 5 and 6 of the book *Why People Play* (Ellis, M. J., Prentice-Hall, 1973), this review, written by Scholtz, takes that original work and extends it in two ways. Firstly, Scholtz being multilingual has brought very old German and Dutch ideas on this topic into the English literature. Secondly, the overview reaches further into the contemporary psychological literature and fleshes out the ideas by reference to work in other areas.

The next chapter, *Attributes Modulating Preference*, gets right down to an important theme that ran through experiment after experiment. It deals with the work that had at its core the choices made by children as to which object they wished to play with. In many studies many potential play objects were simultaneously presented, thus forcing choices. The purpose was to disentangle the attributes of the objects that modulated the children's preferences as expressed by their interactions with them. The importance of these preferences for objects in the physical environment has a natural point of application for those interested in optimizing the physical environments of children; those persons concerned with the design of school programs, playgrounds, and toys.

The next chapter, *Activity of Children*, stems directly from the work honoring the mandate to study the informal lives of normal and exceptional children. This work deals essentially with activity and hyperactivity.

The next chapter deals with *Creativity and Boredom*; two concepts that are closely allied to play. They are treated together because the methods employed to study creativity and boredom had similar elements. In a sense the chapter asks how do children deal with boredom; what responses or strategies do they create to fill an information void. Secondly, it adds some data to the body of knowledge bearing on the question "why are some children more creative than others?"

The last short chapter, *Review and Preview* tries to summarize the contents and show what the future holds.

It is important that we acknowledge those that made this work possible. Firstly, the founders of the laboratory—R. E. Herron, now of Texas Medical Research Center, Baylor University, was the first Director. Herron with W. P. Hurder, Superintendent of the Adler Zone Center, Illinois Department of Mental Health, and Director, Institute for Research of Exceptional Children, obtained the first major infusion of funds that started the work on motor performance. They were wise enough to allow the broadening of the laboratory's function to include play behavior. They work contained herein was nearly all conducted during the time when M. J. Ellis was the Director of the laboratory, although the work had some of its roots in discussions and decisions made in Herron's time.

The work was continued under the sponsorship of three agencies whose heads worked in concert to encourage and provide for the work. The Illinois Department of Mental Health through its research funding programmes supported the work financially via J. G. Langan, the second Superintendent of the Adler Zone Center. We were supported academically, and to some extent financially, through the enthusiastic support of A. V. Sapora, head of the Department of Recreation, University of Illinois. Finally, we were housed and garnered some support from the Children's Research Center, University of Illinois. The second Director of the Children Research Center, R. L. Sprague, not only supported us but with his research team joined us in several studies as co-workers. We also want to publicly acknowledge the debt the laboratory owes to the workers of the Statistical Services Unit associated with the Digital Computer Center at the University of Illinois. This patience and help, especially that of Joe Kolman, was exemplary.

Finally, as authors, we both would like to acknowledge that our respective universities have allowed and encouraged us to complete this monograph. The work has been difficult to complete with Scholtz at Potchefstroom

University for Christian Higher Education in the Republic of South Africa and Ellis, at Dalhousie University in Canada. However, at a critical stage in the preparation of the manuscript we were jointly accorded writing facilities and hospitality at the Windgate Institute, Israel, for which we thank G. Weingarten and U. Simri. Our thanks also go to T. Pottie who typed the manuscript and to D. Pepler who criticised and proofread.

M. J. Ellis

G. J. L. Scholtz

Chapter 1 / **Introduction and Methods**

Introduction

The nature-nurture issue has languished, and the notion that an individual results from the interaction of inherited determinants and the effects of the individual's unique environment and experience holds sway. Explaining play requires such an interactionist view. It is the behavior emitted by individuals temporarily freed from the constraints of external rewards and punishments and is presumed to be maintained by forces wired into the individuals themselves. The exact nature of the behavior is conditioned by previous experience. Thus inherited mechanisms give rise through their interaction with the realities of experience to play behaviors.

Older theories have been rejected. They required reference to a function beyond the present. Play existed to recapitulate the past or prepare for the future, yet we are now happy to argue that play is behavior satisfying in itself. Dickerson claims that ". . . play should be viewed from the stand point of its role in the present rather than its function for the future or as a reflection of the past (1973)."

The nature of the intrinsic forces which sustain play behaviors when other consequences are removed has been argued elsewhere (Ellis, 1973). This monograph describes work organized, in large part, around the notion that individuals have received, via their germ plasm, a propensity to seek information from the environment. Traffic with the environment that produces information is rewarding. The behaviors that produce information,

1

exploration, investigation, and manipulation are commonly recognized as play.

Information is dependent on what is known, which in turn is dependent on experiences. Thus all that remains to complete the argument is to show why information-seeking is critical enough to be stabilized across individuals by inheritance and to demonstrate the mechanisms that differentially reward information-producing responses. As higher animals and humans have evolved, the environmental niches they occupied have become more complex. Survival was still dependent on adaptation to circumstances, but in these complex niches circumstances were sometimes subject to change. If the change was more rapid than the germ plasm could accommodate, then changes within the living individual were required. Once the structure was laid down, the only remaining avenue for change lay in the modification of behavior. Individuals who learned survived. Eventually there was profit in capitalizing on the capacity to change and in living in settings characterized by change.

For those species dependent on their capacity to exploit change the propensity to engage in activity that sought information elaborated and varied their behaviors. Responsiveness to novelty became of critical selective importance. This explains the process that selected individuals with a mechanism that rewarded an active and curious engagement with the world; but it does not describe that mechanism.

The mechanism that actually rewards the selection of responses that reach into the unknown has proved more difficult to find. It is easy to theorize about possible mechanisms. We have the words to think about mechanisms, but finding the actual structures which sort and selectively reinforce one set of responses rather than another has proved elusive. Some of the work presented here bears on that, but in the final analysis, play can be dealt with adequately without explaining every link in the causal chain. For example, it is still not known exactly how sweet-tasting substances interact with an individual's structure to reinforce the behaviors that preceded their ingestion. Despite this we have no conceptual difficulty in dealing with the notion that sweets can function as rewards.

Play behavior, then, requires an interactionist view of development. It is rooted in the biology of our survival and is expressed by individuals in the face of their experience. These views of play are more carefully treated elsewhere (Ellis, 1973, Chapters 5 and 6) and sustain all the work treated in this monograph.

Play appears early in life, and its prevention seriously disturbs the social and cognitive development of the individual. The literature on child and primate development is extensive, and it paints a picture of two kinds of pressures exerted on behavior. The prepotent pressure of survival in our society exacts from an individual the capacity to emit necessary responses to given situations. The second pressure is rooted in the interaction of the unique set of events the individual has experienced with the need to generate information. The first pressure, with its criterion behaviors, leads to our homogenization. The second allows heterogeneity. If you like, the first is the pressure of work, and the second that of play.

The criterion behaviors are critical. The consequences of ignoring gravity, for instance, produce an instant reminder. Normal people learn a large variety of balancing skills and behave homogeneously with regard to gravity. In the patterning of our social lives there are similar pressures to produce behavioral homogeneity. For example, children are consistently enjoined to eat in a way considered appropriate to the family and subculture; eating behaviors are homogenized. As a result there are typical behaviors.

Not all responses are consistently pressured by a complex of social and environmental pressures to produce common predictable repertoires of responses. Many responses fall outside this complex but still change the individual. As these unique experiences accumulate, the resulting behaviors are increasingly heterogeneous among individuals, although for any given individual they might follow a pattern. This behavior is usually seen as falling outside the constraints of the social and physical environments and does not pose a threat to their orderliness. Thus it is often seen as trivial and is not studied. However, this class of behavior is critical in the long view. The survival of species occupying plastic environmental niches depends on it. It is equally important to study the systems that modulate the plastic, flexible, creative, or playful behavior that, as a by-product, increases the chances of individuals' being able to manage the requirements of a changing setting.

During the 1960s the importance of using the methods of science to disentangle the structure of informal behavior in children was nourished by the intersection of two problems facing those caring for children; manpower and hyperactivity. It was becoming increasingly difficult to honor the expectations of the high-quality institutional care for children. Our expectations for that care in schools, hospitals, day-care centers, children's homes, and mental health clinics had run away from our social capacity to deliver it. There was an increased willingness to explore the role that informal settings played in the life of the child. Furthermore there was an increasing concern with the activity of the child. Notions of hyperactivity had reared their heads, and the hyperactive syndrome, although not understood, was fashionable. Research on activity levels among children was therefore interesting, and moneys were obtained to support a series of studies that dealt with the question of how to study the activity of children who were presumably honoring the effects of their own unique experiences in their play. The application of science could not begin until there were methods available to generate numbers describing the behavior. That story is the point of the remainder of this chapter. But before beginning to discuss the procedures themselves, critical background issues for the study of play, reactivity, and habituation must be dealt with.

Reactivity

Studying the behavior of mammals in natural settings is a difficult process. The very act of observing or introducing a measuring device is usually obtrusive. Animals or people have survived as a species, by attending carefully to new elements in their environment and behaving circumspectly towards them. Thus the behavioral tendencies of the higher mammals are finely tuned to react to novel elements like experimenters and their apparatus.

Reactivity is the name given to the process whereby a subject's behavior is changed by the very nature of the researchers' arrangements to observe or manipulate the subject's behavior. Thus reactivity is a constant threat to the validity of an experiment and is of special concern to those studying play or informal settings. It cannot be controlled for by using a control group to provide a baseline, because that baseline must result from observations also. The researcher is always faced with the question, "In what way has the behavior I would like to describe as typical for the population or species been necessarily changed by the processes involved in measuring it?" The answer cannot be insured against the residual doubt that the behavior was changed in some way. The scientist can only struggle to eliminate as many reactive intrusions into the setting as possible. There can be no guarantee that the researchers were successful. The consumers of the research must *judge* whether the reactive intrusion was *unlikely* to have changed the behavior enough to disallow generalization of the findings to behavior emitted in the absence of an experiment.

Although these issues have been understood for centuries, they have not prevented social and behavioral scientists from making many errors. For example work-study scientists faced with the process of quantifying and evaluating normal work habits found that workers modify their performance when under observation. The presence of a person with a stopwatch and clipboard is soon recognized, and the work patterns are changed to serve the workers' own interests. They work more slowly, observe safety precautions, follow the rules, and thwart the intent of the observer to find out what they usually do. It is said that skilled workers possess three sets of skills, one set when they are working naturally, another when demonstrating to an apprentice, and a third when observed by the management. This is reactivity at work.

The question becomes more serious when the setting is carefully managed to become as unlike a natural setting as possible. Laboratory settings are arranged to hold constant most of the events that vary in a natural setting. In fact the fewer the variables, the better the experiment. Thus the less natural the setting becomes, the greater is the obtainable scientific precision concerning relations between a particular variation in a setting and changes in behavior. *But* at the same time, the greater the threat is to the likelihood that that is how people or animals will behave in their normal settings.

The issue of reactivity and its effects on experimental results has attracted some attention in the last decade. Argyris (1968) points out several traps inherent in the reactivity of experiments on people that derive from the social structure of the experimental setting. The requirements of science impose upon the experiment, regardless of the issue being investigated, an intrusive and necessary subjugation of the subject to the experiment. The experimenter controls the setting, decides what the subjects need to know, and constrains them to respond to certain classes of events in certain ways. They either acquiesce, often beneficently trying to help the experiment along, or struggle in various ways to subvert the experiment. The subjects rarely behave naturally. The social psychology of the experimental setting and the reactivity inherent in using people to do research on people has been breezily surveyed by Martens (1973) in his article "People errors in people experiments."

"People errors" can often be avoided by hiding the observer from the observed, an old principle well understood and obvious to naturalists and hunters. There are two other classes of strategies that avoid this kind of reactivity. They also involve not letting the subjects know they are being observed. Of these two, one involves using instruments rather than people to generate the observations, and the other involves observing the traces of a behavior after it has occurred.

The last set of strategies is intriguingly dealt with by Webb *et al.* (1966) in their book, *Unobtrusive measures: Nonreactive research in the social sciences.* Here the authors catalog a series of principles and examples of procedures used by behavioral scientists to avoid or at least minimize the reactivity of their research and increase the likely validity of their efforts. They bring together examples of ingenious measures and procedures that have been used to study the common or typical elements of human behavior. They deal with measurements like the frequency of replacing floor tiles in front of a museum exhibit as an indicator of its popularity, or the height of finger smears on a glass as indicators of with whom the exhibit was popular. Webb *et al.* required a book to make their case, and it is readily available, so the two examples above are sufficient to give the flavor of the ingenuity necessary.

Using instruments to register the changes in the setting produced by behavior rather than using our own sense organs is another obvious ploy. Contemporary technology, given its miniaturization, often allows the instrumentation of the behavior so that nonreactive intrusions into the setting can be made. This chapter deals with some procedures developed to enable this to take place. However, there is no one convenient source for all the instruments developed to convert elements of behavior to signals that can be dealt with by the experimenter. An introduction to this kind of instrumentation can be found in Sidowski (1966).

Instrumenting a setting, albeit unobtrusively, is plagued by another trade-off. Instruments are responsive to very narrowly defined sets of events. They respond to changes in pressure, light intensity, temperature, etc., and quite often narrow ranges of change at that. They are usually highly reliable within their range of sensitivity but necessarily unresponsive to changing circumstances. Human observers on the other hand can respond admirably to a very wide range of inputs, can recognize patterns and change the rules. However, they get tired, lose interest, and are subject to the social pressures in the setting; as a result they often inadvertently change the rules governing the relationships between the behavioral event and the score, and subvert the experiment.

This debate over the use of observers or instruments is an important one. The different characteristics of the human observer and the instrumentation available for an experiment must be dealt with. The limitations of both must be accounted for in deciding how to generate scores that describe behaviors. Two excellent debates of the issue exist in the literature (Whitfield, 1967; Runkel and McGrath, 1972).

To summarize, the processes of science require the generation of measures or scores that describe the events of concern. Generating procedures for tying scores to events is fraught with difficulty. The process of measuring itself is likely to be reactive. When people are used to control and measure the behavior, the experimental situation becomes a social situation, subject to a complex set of social interactions. Using instruments to bypass these intrusive interactions raises the specter of rigid measuring equipment's mechanically recording events without any capacity to recognize the patterns and changing circumstances vital to the interpretation of the data; something easily undertaken by a human. All solutions are potentially damaging to the validity of the experiment, and the art inherent in being a scientist involves dealing with the trade-offs.

Measuring Play

Against a background of concern for these issues the research on activity and play behavior of children at the Motor Performance and Play Research Laboratory was begun. The early research was not guided by any clear theoretical notions as to why a mammal would be particularly reactive to novel and changing elements in the environment. The role of exploration, investigation, manipulation, and fantasy in ensuring the survival of species and individuals by helping them to accommodate rapidly to changing circumstances had not then been clearly stated. However, the delicacy of play and activity in informal settings was understood, since the determinants of play were presumed to lie within the individual actor.

In the beginning the research was directed at what was called activity in the free-range. The ecologist's term was borrowed to avoid the difficulties perceived in defining and explaining play at that time. The behavior was presumed to be relatively free of directly imposed constraints to behave in certain ways. A play setting seemed to be characterized by the availability of choices.

It was believed, however, that the choices made by an individual were not spontaneous or random, but were modulated by the orderly processes residing in each child and his or her own experiences. The order inherent in the children's behavior had to be preserved, not subverted, by the experimental process.

The Play Research Laboratory

The corollary to the notion that mammals are unusually attentive to novel elements in their environments is that they are inattentive to familiar elements. The habituation to new things is usually rapid and works to the advantage of the scientist. So long as the intrusions into the setting are familiar and static, then the behavior of concern will be unaffected.

Exploiting this, a setting in which it was possible to make the necessary arrangements for observing and measuring of activity was established as part of the normal experiences of some children. A laboratory adjacent to the Children's Research Center preschool was converted into a playroom in 1967. Every child came to the playroom every day as part of his or her normal routine, and the setting itself soon became nonreactively familiar.

The playroom was stocked with a variety of items selected because they were modular in design and allowed a very large variety of combinations. Thus the contents of the physical setting were changeable. The apparatus was designed to elicit gross motor activity and was changed routinely about once a month (i.e., about every 20 visits), and its complexity was increased towards the end of the year. Thus a situation was created in which it was normal to visit the playroom daily, and it was normal for the playroom arrangement to change every now and again. After habituation to the setting, only two things remained necessary for the scientific study of activity in this informal setting: a set of hypotheses about the effects of the arrangements of physical and social setting on that activity, and the development of nonreactive procedures for quantifying the activity of the children.

These two needs are intimately interlinked and are the subject of many a "chicken or egg" debate in science. There is no point in having a procedure if it doesn't help to answer a question, but then it's often of little use posing a good question if there are no procedures to make an answer possible. At the Children's Research Center the procedures, theory, and hypotheses were developed side by side in a tangled process sustained by a belief in the need to understand informal activity.

Recording Play Behavior

The first recording procedures in our laboratory were undertaken by Wuellner in 1967. He filmed the playroom using a wide-angle lens on a 16-mm camera mounted on a tripod in the doorway. The procedure was highly reactive at first. The strange person, equipment, and noise excited considerable attention. Surprisingly this reactivity did not seem to persist beyond a few minutes, since the playroom and its contents were more enticing than the filmmaker and camera. Although habituation to this setting was rapid, the system had many disadvantages. The whole room was not included. It seriously disturbed the children's behavior immediately after its introduction. Therefore this system could not be used to study the behavior immediately following the children's entry into the room, it could not be left set up in the doorway, and it did not resolve the problem of how to transform the observed behavior in the room to numbers. The filming was a success, however, because it recorded some play, and its study crystallized the problems involved.

Wuellner's first analysis tried merely to describe the patterns of movement from one piece of apparatus to another. He attempted to improve on the procedures described by Dow in 1933, who, using scaled plans of four different playgrounds, traced the movement of a subject from minute to minute. The film record allowed the series of events to be rerun and eliminated errors inherent in a real-time analysis. In addition, the time-base and a large number of exposures per minute allowed a much more fine-grained analysis.

A review of the literature (Wuellner, 1969; Wuellner, Witt, and Herron, 1970) showed how others had partially solved similar problems. Swinton in 1934 used a roof-mounted time-lapse camera to study the use of a playground. Ellis and Pryor (1959) crisscrossed a room at 2-foot intervals with photoelectric cells to quantify activity of children with pronounced neuropathology. Then Hutt, Hutt, and Ounsted (1963) used the tiles on the floor to the same effect in a tape-recorded description of the content of the play behavior they observed in their playroom. These elements were simultaneously incorporated in one system made possible for the first time by improvements in photographic systems and computer software.

What was needed now was a system that recorded the behavior so that the analysis did not have to be conducted in real time, that minimized reactivity, and that was objective, versatile, and inexpensive to operate.

The Fisheye Camera System

To satisfy these requirements a time-lapse camera system was built that photographed the whole room from above. The location of the children in space was determined by taping a 1-yard grid to the floor to provide a set of coordinates. The coordinates of the children in each sample or photograph became the data from which a set of computer programs produced a variety of measures describing the children's activity. The camera system was first described by Wuellner, Witt, and Herron in 1968 (1970) and the computer software by Herron and Frobish (1969).

The camera was a 35-mm Nikon F that was semipermanently mounted on the ceiling 9 feet from the floor. To allow the whole play area to be included in the image, an Accura accessory fisheye lens was fitted to a 50-mm, f 1.4 Nikkor lens. The focal length of the combined lens was 7.5 mm, and an angle of acceptance of 180° was produced. Since the camera was suspended 9 feet above a floor area approximately 22 × 29 feet, the "hemispherical" image included the complete functional volume of the space in which the children could play.

To allow more than 36 exposures, the camera was fitted with a body containing an accessory motor drive and large storage cassettes that permitted remote triggering, automatic exposure, and shutter reset. Film wind-on was controlled by an ancillary timer built especially for the purpose. This was essentially a synchronous motor with different gearing systems to produce the triggering pulse of current at different intervals. It contained a counter to display the number of exposure pulses and was started and stopped by hand.

Since a typical play session was 15 minutes and the camera body held 250 exposures, a sampling interval of 10 seconds was chosen arbitrarily for the early studies. It allowed 90 frames for each play session, and allowed two sessions to be recorded in each cassette. Data produced later showed that this sampling rate is too slow for high fidelity. But hindsight is always clearer than foresight, and the early studies had been completed by the time that data were at hand. A typical image produced by the camera system is shown in Fig. 1.1.

The film was then developed and printed on a strip of 5-inch-wide glossy paper. The location of each child was recorded by the scorer. This was a time-consuming process that required recognizing the children and assigning coordinates to the position of the approximate center of gravity of each of the children above the grid taped to the floor. The scorer, Wuellner, tried to estimate this to .2 yard.

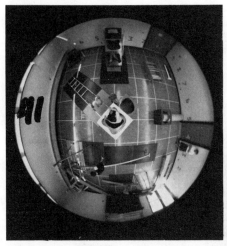

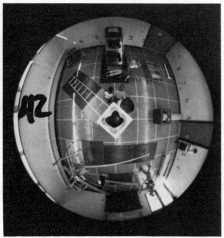

Fig. 1.1: Typical frames produced by the early camera system.

This process involved pattern recognition, recognizing a particular child, and counting coordinates and interpolating. It was theoretically possible to automate the assignment of coordinates at that time, but the subtle nature of automatic pattern recognizing involved in identifying one three- or four-year-old child was not possible without highly reactive manipulations of their clothing. Haith (1966) had described a system for reading position data on a plane surface after the objects to be positioned had been recognized. This system involved a series of fine wires stretched over the screen on which the film record was projected. The scorer touched the image with a probe, and the activated horizontal and vertical wires triggered a card punch. Unfortunately, the by-now familiar distortion introduced by the fisheye lens would have required the introduction of expensive and complex compensatory curves into the wires of Haith's system to restore the plane geometry of the image. The advantages of the fisheye lens brought with them the disadvantages of manual recording, but this was but a small addition to the work involved in recognition.

Humans being what they are, there were many errors. Wuellner reported that of the 1080 "X" and "Y" coordinates in an inter-observer reliability sample, 23% were not in complete agreement. Intra-observer performance errors looked worse with 32% disagreement. However, 98% of the errors were only .2 yard in size, and the reliability coefficient using this procedure exceeded +.98. The use of .2 yard in the position location procedures was spuriously precise, and in further studies location was assigned to 1-yard squares.

Scores Produced by the Fisheye System

This study, the first to produce useful data, provided the opportunity to deal with the problem of using high-speed computation to reduce the masses of coordinates describing the position in time of all the children in the room. The Herron and Frobish study (1969) presented for the first time a set of indicators or descriptors of the activity of individual children and the apparatus utilization patterns of the playing group. (See Appendix A.)

The Herron and Frobish (1969) study broke new ground by producing four classes of descriptors of the behavior of the children, derived from the position × time data. Computer software was designed to produce graphic display of the movement patterns of each child by means of a sequential graphic plot of their changing positions; descriptors of the overall locomotor

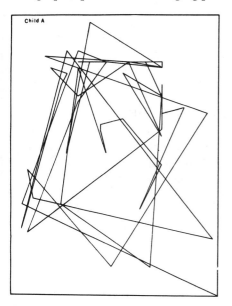
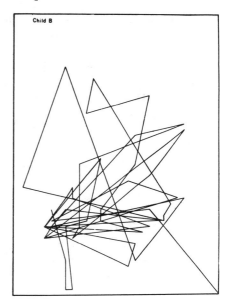

Fig. 1.2: Plots of the paths of children during play sessions.

activity of the child; descriptors of the play equipment utilization by the group; and descriptors of the relationships among the positions of children.

The immediate appeal of using the Calcomp (*California Computer Prod-ucts*) plotter to produce a representation of the path followed by the children soon waned. The obvious differences in patterns of behavior, represented by individual two-dimensional trajectories, were not readily reducible to num-bers for objective comparison. Attributes of the patterns, like their concentra-tion, "jerkiness," or angularity, were better described by other measures. Calcomp plots, although eyecatching, were never used in an experiment. However, the other three sets of derived scores were used and progressively refined through a series of experiments. To simplify this text, the arithmetic derivation of all the scores used as dependent variables in all studies is given in Appendix A. So, in the remainder of the text only the verbal labels will be used to describe the attribute of the behavior being measured.

The measurements of locomotion of each child in the room were all derived changes in location from frame to frame of the film record. The differ-ences between pairs of X and Y coordinates taken from one frame to the next were used as the sides of a triangle, and the Pythagorean theorem was used to determine the straight-line distance covered (the hypotenuse) in the interval. The series of distances covered from frame to frame (the sample intervals) were used to generate scores describing the movement of the child. Thus adding them produced an estimate of the total distance moved. Count-ing the number of samples in which there was no movement was an indicator of quiescence. Dividing the total distance moved by the number of intervals in which there was movement, the complement of the previous measure, provided a measure of velocity. The standard deviation of the distances gave indication of the "jerkiness" or variability of movement of individuals. Other scores were developed for particular purposes, but these give the general picture of the kinds of scores that could be derived from the individual posi-tion × time data that described the locomotor activity of individual children. The individual measurements were then used as the dependent variables in analyses of the effects various manipulations had on this aspect of the chil-dren's behavior. The research on activity and hyperactivity that this system made possible is dealt with in Chapter 4.

The differential use of the various items of play apparatus in the play-room was determined by coding which object each child was using for each frame. Counting the frequencies in various ways generated indicators of equipment usage. In the early Wuellner study the equipment was defined as the object plus a limited territory surrounding it defined by two X and two Y coordinates. The computer was programmed to test which area each child was playing in for each frame, and the frequencies were tallied to produce a usage score for each object.

Later the use of the computer to assign a number to the equipment being used in a frame was discontinued. The observer could see which items the child was playing on, and movable equipment could be coded easily. Although apparently less sophisticated, the coding procedure was improved by having the human recognize the patterns and the machine do the arithmetic. The last few studies of equipment usage went one stage further and coded the intensity of use of the item (Gramza, 1972). Usage was scored as no use, tentative use or touching, and complete usage when the apparatus bore the weight of the child.

The equipment-use scores also were used to derive different measurements. Simple frequency counts were used to differentiate the popularity of different items within and across children. The number of different visits to a play object and the duration of each visit could be derived simply to indicate the power of an item to attract the children and to maintain their interest with it. Then the variability of individual children's use of the items was used to produce a measure of their distractibility under different circumstances. These scores describing differences in usage made possible the series of experiments on preference described in Chapter 3 and contributed to the study of hyperactive children by reflecting their distractibility, which is discussed in Chapter 4.

The remaining class of scores to be derived from the film record involved the computation of the relative positions of the children to each other on a given frame. Here the Pythagorean theorem was used to determine the distance between two children. Using the differences between pairs of X and Y coordinates for two different children, the hypotenuse connecting them represented the distance between the two children at the time the frame was exposed. The computer was programmed to solve the equation for all the distances among children on a frame and to repeat the process for the total number of frames. Adding the distances, appropriately, produced such derived measures as the relative dispersion of the group, the mean between child distance, and the relative isolation of each child. In essence these measures provided an indicator of who tended to play with whom. Much after the fashion of a sociogram, this procedure used the actual behavior of the children to construct a "spatiogram" numerically describing the clustering of children within the group under differing circumstances. This technique was little used but remains a useful and objective way of quantifying a particular aspect of group behavior. It should be of use to those now studying the proximity of individuals in a new area of study called proxemics.

Testing the Fisheye System

Once the procedures were developed, it was necessary to check the validity and reliability of the system. Studies were then undertaken using the activity measures and the equipment-use measures.

The effect of assuming that children were moving in straight lines between successive positions was tested by Craig (1969). In this study the camera was run at 2-second intervals. The total distance moved in a series of 7-minute sessions (7.5 minutes required all 225 exposures available in the camera body) was computed, and the 2-second interval score was taken as criterion. The analysis was rerun, dropping out alternate data points. This functionally degraded the data to simulate a run of samples made at 4-second intervals. The process was repeated to produce 8-, 10-, and 16-second intervals. These estimates of the same behavior were then compared with the criterion estimate produced from the train of 2-second samples to determine at what point the trade-off between economy and validity could be maximized. Fig. 1.3 shows the outcome.

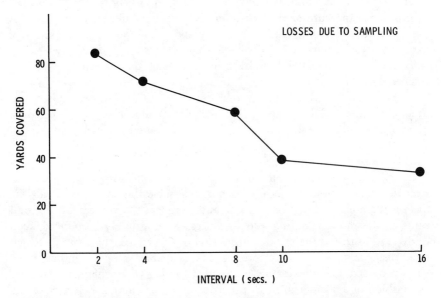

Fig. 1.3: Loss in accuracy due to reduction of sampling rate.

The degrading of the sampling interval progressively reduced the apparent distance covered to a 10-second sample and then leveled off. This is easy to explain. The pathways of the children were not linear, and sampling at the highest rate caused least distance to be lost by the straight-line assumption that cut off the corners of their individual paths. At the 10-second sampling interval the amount cut-off approximately equaled that registered, and serial dependency of position in successive samples had been lost. Each position was so separated in time that the process was apparently random, producing only slight further degradation when the sample interval was pushed out to 16 seconds. Thus the validity of the measure diminished as the rate of sampling was reduced.

The planned experiments called for comparison of the effects of treatments on activity. Therefore, the reduction of the estimated distance covered was not crucial, so long as it reduced the distance reliably. If it merely subtracted a constant rather than interacting with the movement patterns of individual children, then a relatively inexpensive sampling rate could still be used. To check this, a set of distances covered for each interval for each child at each sampling rate was correlated with the criterion rate of one sample every 2 seconds. Fig. 1.4 shows the percent of variance in common and the

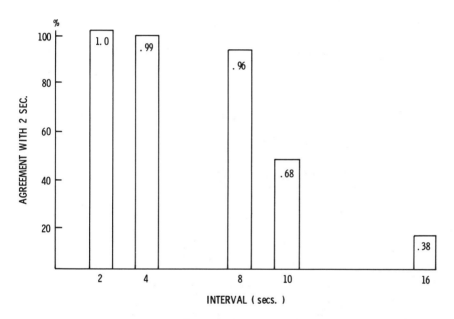

Fig. 1.4: Correlation of distance data produced by progressively degraded samples with the criterion sample.

product moment correlations between sets of estimated distances moved. Halving the number of samples to one every 4 seconds reliably reduced the distance moved. The distribution of the distances moved by children relative to one another was not disturbed ($r = .99$). The degradation subtracted a constant. The same was essentially true when the rate was halved again to one sample every 8 seconds ($r = .98$). There was a marked drop off in reliability, however, when the sample rate was dropped to one every

10 seconds. The correlation coefficient r was now only .68, and by reducing the sampling rate again to one very 16 seconds, the relative standing of individuals was so disturbed that less than 20% of variance in the estimated distance moved by the children at the 2-second interval was accounted for. To be conservative while still reducing the cost of operating the system to one half, a sampling interval of 4 seconds was used in all studies thereafter.

To study the validity of the equipment-usage measurements, Witt and Wuellner (1969) video taped the usage of an item of apparatus, a ladder leaning against a stack of two 2-foot cubes directly beneath the camera. They videotaped five 15-minute sessions simultaneously; the camera was being exposed at 10-second intervals.

The continuous 15-minute video tape was timed to the nearest second to produce the total duration of usage of the ladder and cube item by six children. The film sample record was scored also, and estimates of duration (total visit time) were made by multiplying the number of frames in which the apparatus was being used by 10 seconds, the sampling interval. Table 1.1 shows that the camera system was validly estimating duration, but was adding approximately a sampling interval of 11.3 seconds to the duration.

Table 1.1

VALIDITY OF CAMERA SYSTEM ESTIMATES OF EQUIPMENT USAGE

| Child | Camera System | | Video System |
	Frequency	Frequency × 10 = Duration secs.	Duration secs.
1	15	150	148
2	33	330	308
3	18	180	183
4	18	180	161
5	11	110	99
6	30	300	283
		$\bar{X} = 208.3$	$\bar{X} = 197$

The effect of sampling rate on the equipment-usage measurements was also checked using data from a study that was published later (Karlsson and Ellis, 1972). The frequency with which a child used each of 13 pieces of equipment on four open areas during a 15-minute period was calculated using sampling rates of 4, 8, 16, and 32 seconds. Separate chi-squared analyses were run for each subject in each session at each sampling rate. In every case, (of about 68 cases) nonsignificant chi-squares were obtained, indicating that the patterns of equipment use were not significantly altered by the sampling rate. The increase in sampling interval tended to drop out the items that were infrequently used. For example, at the 8-second sampling interval approximately 10% of the pieces of equipment shown as being used at the 4-second interval did not show any use. This was a useful attribute. Those interested in popular apparatus with high utilization rates could set a sampling interval that would purge their data automatically of unpopular items. On the other hand, the more rapid sampling rates allowed a more complete description of all usages.

These studies led Korb (1968) to advance a "kinetic theory of activity." He postulated that the activity estimates produced by this system were not simply a matter of the children's own urge to be active but were conditioned by the opportunities to run. The room was small, and the paths were obstructed by the apparatus and other children. The peak velocity of any child was therefore limited. Thus, the selection of a sampling interval should be specific to the crowding of a particular-sized room. Activity would be inversely conditioned by the size of the room and the crowding of the space. Korb recognized that there were limits to the application of this notion to behavior, but he argued for a careful checking of the sampling interval for each play area in which this sampling system was used. Different-sized rooms, different arrangements, and different numbers of children would require different sampling rates. A simple procedure for checking this has been demonstrated.

Improving the Fisheye System

Several procedural disadvantages remained to be dealt with. (1) It was difficult to recognize individual children, and this was necessary if the individual patterns of play were to be dealt with. (2) The photographic procedures were expensive. (3) The grid taped to the floor was reactive; the children used the lines to play on.

These problems were relatively simple to overcome, and a paper by Wuellner, Witt, and Korb (1969) reported the solutions. Identifying the children was relatively simple once the clothing of each child could be recognized. This was accomplished by photographing the children as a group in a different setting but on the same day as the study. Then the teachers positively identified each child on the polaroid print, and it was filed to serve as a guide when a particular session was to be scored. This procedure avoided the necessity for attaching identifying marks that would be visible in a photo image no matter what attitude the child adopted. The combination of each child's physical characteristics plus his or her specific clothing allowed highly reliable identification.

When the film record was printed on 3 1/2" × 5" glossy paper, it was expensive, cumbersome, and, because of the small size, difficult to score. Furthermore the bulk processing of "tri-X" film required a shutter speed of 1/30 to 1/60th of a second, a speed which failed to stop the motion of the playing children. The solution came from switching to the production of a positive-image filmstrip which was projected to produce the image to be scored. Several advantages accrued. The two-stage process, from negative to positive image strip, produced much greater tonal ranges permitting easier recognition of the children. The developing and printing processes required a shorter exposure time, eliminating blurring due to movement. The positive projection functionally enlarged the image by projecting it from a greater distance using conventional 35-mm strip projectors. Finally the cost of these images was 2.4¢ per exposure (see Appendix B for technical details of the photographic procedures), far less than the 7.2¢ per exposure required to produce glossy prints.

The remaining problem of adding the coordinate grid was now simply solved. The images of the playroom were projected on a grid of coordinates of convenient size. Landmarks were used to orientate the images to the grid exactly. The grid lines were distorted to compensate for the fisheye lens's distortion by photographing, through the same fisheye lens, a rectilinear grid of the same proportions as the grid that was formerly taped to the playroom floor (see Fig. 1.5). Thus, a procedure for nonreactively recording the activ-

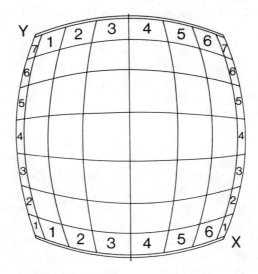

Fig. 1.5: The coordinate grid showing the distortions introduced by the fisheye lens.

ity of a group of children playing together in a play area while preserving their identity was developed. The physical elements of the system were so satisfactory that they were left unchanged for the remainder of the program. However, modifications of the software used to derive dependent variables from the raw position/time data continued to the end, as different variables were evolved to satisfy the needs of particular experiments.

Other Activity Recording Systems

Other systems were explored while the fisheye camera system was being developed. These efforts resulted in three activity measurement systems involving fundamentally different approaches: (1) The development of a telepedometer which was a micro-miniaturized system for telemetering the force of impact of the heel during locomotion. (2) A multi-channel, heart-rate telemetry system which recorded each heart beat of each child, providing an indicator of energy expended. (3) A helmet and sampling system to sample the expired gases of the child necessary to compute energy expenditure was developed. This allowed a child to range freely without having to wear an obtrusive face mask. Only the heart-rate telemetry system was used extensively in the research of the laboratory, and the others although potentially useful were not exploited. Though not used in the Illinois program, all three systems will be described since they might be useful in others.

The Telepedometer

The telepedometer was developed by Herron and Ramsden (1967) and Ramsden (1967). This system involved building a pressure transducer and FM transmitter into the heel of the child's shoe. The components were miniature elements potted in a resilient material with a magnetic switch and a tuning device accessible to a thin screwdriver via a strategically bored hole in the front surface of the heel. Field trials of the telepedometer showed that it had a range of 100 feet (this could be extended by the addition of an aerial), was highly stable, had a battery life of 100 hours, and survived normal wear for over 100 hours. Further, the patterns of walking and running were distinguishable when the signals were written on a polygraph (Herron and Weir, 1968).

The application of the device to the problems of concern in the laboratory at that time were difficult. Although once installed, the device was nonreactive; each device had to be custom installed into a specific shoe of the subject. The children under study from the Department of Mental Health habitually wore sneakers, did not like shoes, or quickly outgrew them. Coupling these daily difficulties to the problem of making inferences about play and activity patterns from the series of transmitted pulses, it can be seen that for the Motor Performance and Play Research Laboratory the telepedometer became an interesting toy, but not a significant working device. Its potential has not been exploited. It would be useful in studies of adults where the nonreactive quantification of locomotor elements of work is important and in studies of the very long-term activity patterns of people in a free range.

The Heart-Rate Telemetry System

In a further effort to describe the activity of children, directly but unobtrusively, a multi-channel heart-rate telemetry system was developed. Heart rate has been a popular dependent variable in the literature for measuring the level of energy expenditure. Activity is measured indirectly utilizing an inference that the excursions of the heart rate from resting levels are related to the intensity and recency of antecedent energy expenditures. The heart rate can be used as an index of the energy cost of the recent activity of the child. Since the research involved the investigation of activity patterns the use of heart rate seemed appropriate.

The need to reduce the reactivity of any system while allowing subjects to range freely in relatively naturalistic settings required unobtrusive, robust, multi-channel telemetry. Further, the transmitters also had to filter out the noise generated by the body movements, while monitoring the energy costs of the very movements that were creating the noise.

Existing transmitter systems were inadequate. They could not withstand the robust play of the children, nor did they filter off the noise, so a new transmitter system was designed. The new transmitter was designed and technical data were published (Geeseman and Wade, 1971 and Appendix C). The transmitters were about half the volume of a pack of cigarettes (1 1/4″ × 2″ × 3/4″) and were mounted on an ordinary belt on the child against the small of the back. In this position it was soon forgotten by the children, and they played as usual when wearing the device.

The small changes in voltage in the chest region that accompany each heart contraction were relayed to an amplifier by means of electrodes stuck to the sternum. The amplified signal was then converted to an FM pulse that was broadcast to a receiver. The received signal was then split and written on a polygraph and recorded on magnetic tape.

These systems were elaborated until they were highly reliable, and four separate systems could be employed simultaneously in the same space. Thus the individual activity of four children playing together in a group could be monitored completely and simultaneously. This telemetry system was used in studies of activity and is the other substantive method underpinning much of the work reported in Chapter 4, "Activity of Children."

There were two practicable systems for describing the activity of free-ranging children—the camera and the heart-rate telemetry systems. The first derived from the children's positions at intervals of less than 10 seconds' locomotor and equipment usage patterns; the second allowed the derivation of mean heart rate for longer intervals, usually 30 seconds. In 1970 Karlsson compared these two systems to determine the degree to which they measured common elements in the behavior of free-ranging children. She ran a very small study in which four children were allowed to play together for 10 minutes in the playroom on three occasions. The play behavior was recorded using the camera and telemetry system simultaneously in the second and third sessions. The camera data were collected at the customary 4-second intervals and should have produced 125 position points per child per session. The heart rates were scored as number of beats per 20-second intervals. Some losses of film and the dislodging of a transmitter reduced the number of camera samples to 115 and the number of paired sets of data to seven, but sufficient data were left to produce reliable correlations.

The simplest correlation was checked first. The Pearson-product moment correlation between the heart rate per 20 seconds and the distance covered in the same interval averaged .24 and ranged from −.03 to .52. This was disturbing at the time, and reasons for the lack of association among the sets of scores were sought. The heart-rate data were then lagged one 20-second interval. It was argued that the energy cost of an activity would not instantaneously modulate the heart rate, and the lag in the physiological system could be accommodated in this way. The Pearson-product moment correlation coefficient was hardly altered. It now averaged .27 and ranged from .09 to .64. It seemed as if the two systems were measuring different parameters.

The study was extended to consider one aspect of equipment use. The heart rates were correlated with a very simple index of equipment use which was presumed to generate the most activity. In the play setting were two 8-foot-high trestles with a cargo net slung between them. The children were scored when they were on this apparatus for three or more of the 4-second intervals during the 20-second heart-rate sample. The point-biserial correlation was low, averaging .09 and ranging from −.28 to .53. When intervals in which the children were moving more than 1.5 yards were added to the trestle and net usage, a new unit of activity was generated. This unit was first used by Witt (1971) and was called a gross energy unit. (See Appendix A.) It was presumed this would express in one compound measure the energy costs involved in moving relatively rapidly or climbing and swinging. It was assumed these were the two most strenuous activities exhibited by the children during a play session. Still, no significant Pearson-product moment correlation resulted; it averaged .12 and ranged from −.35 to .48.

The only remaining question to be resolved by this exercise was the hypothesis that the heart-rate sample of 20 seconds was of too coarse a grain to allow the changes in intensity of activity to manifest themselves in a relationship. Two children's traces were chosen at random, and the heart-rate data were recounted into intervals of 4 seconds. Using the procedure of combining data points of lengths, increases in 4-second increments from 4 through 48 seconds were produced. For one child the correlation increased to a respectable .85 by the time the sample had been lengthened to 48 seconds (mean $r = .47$) but the other remained essentially zero throughout (mean $r = .08$).

The exercise described above indicates clearly that the two methods were measuring different aspects of the play behavior of the children. The camera system measures of activity were not correlated with heart rate, which is considered in the literature to be a measure of work done. The nature of these two classes of measures was refined by this study by Karlsson. The camera system and its software generated measures that are best conceived as descriptions of the content of the behavior of the children. This system described what kinds of things the children did, where they moved, what equipment they used, and who they played with. Presumably the heart-rate telemetry system can be conceived of as a system that expresses in sum the intensity of the antecedent behavioral content. The systems should be used in different kinds of studies: the camera system when it is of interest to know what the children were doing during a period, and the heart-rate system when changes in energy expenditure over time are studied.

Analysis of Respired Gases

The remaining method was developed during the years 1967 to 1971. This emerging system used a helmet rather than a face mask to capture a sample of the expired gases. These gases, when analyzed, can be used, given some assumptions about the metabolic processes of the individual, to make precise estimates of the energy used by the subject. Although this collection and analysis of respired gases is relatively arduous, it provides reliable measures of mobilized energy.

Gas collection usually involves the wearing of a face mask or breathing through a mouthpiece and valve, both of which entail two serious disadvantages. The mouthpieces, valves, and attendant tubing add very significantly to the dead space of the respiratory tract and introduce considerable resistance into the respiratory system. Secondly, wearing the face mask or holding the valve with the teeth are both uncomfortable and extremely limiting and distracting for children. The helmet system was developed to avoid the highly reactive effects of the mask or valve, tubes, and strapping on the behavior of the child. In addition it also served to eliminate additional dead space and resistance since the child was breathing in what was functionally a small ventilated environmental chamber perched on the shoulders. (The advantages and disadvantages of the traditional Douglas Valve and the Helmet System are listed in Appendix D.)

It was argued that wearing a "space helmet" or "football helmet" would be more acceptable to children, especially if the head were free to move inside the helmet. The first stage in this project was undertaken by Wade *et al.* (1971) in our laboratory, who developed further the helmet system reported by the NASA Midwest Experimental Station (Lauer, 1967). Lauer's system involved the connection of the helmet to an on-line analysis system. This constrained the activity of the subject drastically. Wade *et al.* added to the NASA version of the system a sampling device that diverted an aliquot from the air stream containing a mixture of room air and expired gas into small metallized bags designed by Johnson *et al.* (1967). These bags were then taken for gas analysis.

The advance made by Wade *et al.* was that they pioneered a less reactive system that would enable the subject to range freely without the encumbrance of a mask or valve and mouthpiece yet produce the kind of precise energy-expenditure estimates permitted by respired-gas analysis. Furthermore the system was potentially much lighter and less clumsy than the Integrating Motor Pneumo-tachograph (Wolff, 1958) or the Kofranyi-Michaelis respirometer (Consolazio, Johnson and Pecora, 1963), the two extant systems for collecting expired gases in the free range.

The Wade device, when placed in conjunction with a Tissot system, underestimated the values for oxygen consumption by 10 to 20%, but the curves were reliable. The project was continued with because we believed it would be useful to have available a procedure to produce a nonreactive criterion measure of the energy expenditures of children in the free range in order to calibrate the other methods directly. Three members of the lab continued to work on the helmet (Foster, Korb, and Samson), making two more versions, each progressively simpler and lighter.

The third version used a polycarbonate globe that formed the basis of the Apollo manned-space program helmet. The globe was fitted with a plastic-covered foam-rubber collar and rested on the shoulders. At the rear of the helmet a miniature squirrel-cage fan drew air via twin vinyl tubes from the helmet in front of the mouth. Air entered the helmet via holes in the top and near both ears. The subject respired a portion of the air as it flowed through the helmet before being passed on through a simple sampling device that diverted a small proportion of the flow into metalized bags sewn into the lining of a loosely fitting waistcoat.

Foster (1971) undertook a study of the helmet system relative to two well known methods; the Douglas valve and Tissot tank and the Volumeter systems. The same subject was used in repeated and counterbalanced 5-minute periods of resting respiration through the three systems, where volumes of O_2 and CO_2 respired were computed, together with the Respiratory Quotients, using the standard procedures (Consolazio, Johnson, and Pecora, 1963).

When the helmet system was placed on line with a Tissot tank, it was found that the composition of the gases in the sample bags and the Tissot were identical in all but two tests, where the differences were .006 liters per minute (a 4% error for these two cases). The sampling system produced a valid aliquot.

The helmet system was also highly reliable. During the eight repeated tests of the helmet, the sample collection technique drew samples ranging from .125% to .138% of the total volume with an average of .131%. The maximum difference of .013% for a 5-minute test would produce an error of at most .04 liters, an insignificant error when the total volume respired in 5 minutes was 230 to 260 liters. The system was reliable. All that was needed for a reliable operation was the calibration of a particular sampling rate by placing it on line with a Tissot system. In fact the data produced by Foster showed that the helmet system was more reliable than the popular Douglas valve and mask system which produced less reproducible results.

The helmet system took several years to be developed to the point described briefly here and in detail in Appendix E. It had great potential as a calibrator of the other methods; for example, the relationship between calories expended and heart rate for a given child would have enabled a far more satisfactory use of the heart-rate telemetry system. However, the resources of people, time, and money were not available to push this project through. That is the privilege of some other worker, and the point of recording this work for the first time is to prevent someone's having to retrace these steps.

Methods are devoid of the excitement of great leaps into theory, but they often provide the satisfaction of solving small problems. This chapter documents the interlinked methodological advances, some complete and some yet to be finished, some useful and others just interesting toys, that ran alongside the substantive work of the laboratory. As Skinner is reputed to have said, "Science is the search for the dependant variable." This chapter illustrates where we searched and what we found.

Chapter *2* | Theoretical Overview

Introduction

The behavior phenomenon generally identified as "play" is as old as mankind itself. And yet, we know so embarrassingly little about it. Speculations and conjectures as to what play is, and its motivation, date back for much more than 2,000 years. Behavioral scientists have had the luxury of theory, however, only in recent decades and, frankly speaking, efficient and operationally viable theory on play behavior is still in its infancy. But there is hope. Recent research proposes promising explanations and predictions concerning play behavior which will be pursued in some detail in this chapter.

Despite the intent to narrow this treatment we recognize that there is no unique explanation for why children play. A multitude of forces are at work to motivate, mediate, maintain, and direct all behavior. This has to be recognized when searching for those forces that modulate play behavior, and each of these forces has to be identified and weighted. The search for stimulation or arousal by means of playful encounters with the environment and the self is one such force. The scope of this chapter is limited to it.

Stimulus-seeking was dealt with extensively in chapter 5 and 6 of Ellis's book *Why People Play* (1973). The material covered there has not been repeated in detail here, and the reader is referred to it for a more careful treatment of the mechanisms presumed to maintain stimulus-seeking and a discussion of their significance. Since those chapters were written it has become obvious that these attempts to explain stimulus, stimulation, or arousal-seeking behaviors, as these behaviors are variously called, have irritated a host of behavioral scientists. Some behavioral scientists believe that it is not fruitful to go beyond the data at hand, namely the observed values of independent variables and dependent variables, to impute the nature of the causal mechanism that transforms one into the other. To these scientists it is sufficient to establish the relations between sets of data and they are unwilling to speculate or infer what takes place within the individual between stimulus and response. This work can be read by these scientists if they purge the writings of all hypothetical constructs like motive, need, arousal as they go. Given that caution, the majority of this book will be palatable since it deals with the relations between sets of data.

Other scientists are willing to practice a science that includes additions to the data. These people will deal with the hypothetical constructs with the understanding that they are merely our labels for the presumed mediating mechanisms that allow conceptual shortcuts from input to output by recognising that something is going on inside the individual—inside the "black box". These constructs, as their name implies, are inferred mechanisms that are only worthwhile to the extent that they enable humans to think about the data at hand. Association can be demonstrated, but cause can only be inferred. To go beyond the finite sets of data extant to deal simply with the infinite number of possible sets, we believe that it is necessary to leap into prediction. We can do that only by inference. Our survival and success in the world require us to generalize. We believe it worthwhile to go beyond the data and to refine our conceptions of what lies inside the "black box" so that we can deal with events that have yet to take place.

Two Approaches

Viewed historically, two broad overlapping phases in the acquisition and development of knowledge about play can be distinguished. They are the philosophical approach with its origins in antiquity and still a loyal companion of modern thinking, and the descriptive analytic approach that presently dominates the realm of the behavioral sciences. For the sake of parsimony, only that knowledge that relates to the notion at the core of this monograph, that play is an example of stimulus-seeking behavior, will be reviewed. There are other approaches too, but they will not be discussed here, as they were surveyed in the "companion" text by Ellis in 1973.

The Philosophical Approach

The philosophical approach which accommodates most of the classical theories is based on rationalized conjectures and speculation about behavioral phenomena in the real world of play. In this category belong such theories as the surplus energy approach, play as activity-seeking behavior, and play as pleasure-maximizing activity. An overview of these approaches is necessary because they are theoretically related to our explanation of play as arousal-seeking.

The so-called surplus energy approach which presumes to explain the motivation of play is rooted in the writings of the poet Friedrich von Schiller in 1800, in Hermann von Helmholtz's conception of the conservation of energy announced in 1847, and finally in Herbert Spencer's writings in 1855. The theory holds that individuals play in order to spend a surplus of energy accumulated as a result of not having had to expend it in the struggle for survival. This approach has a hydraulic connotation and favors quiescence and behavioral equilibrium as the natural state of being. The prediction derived from the surplus energy approach is simply this: if there is surplus energy available, the individual spends it by playing; if not, the individual prefers quiescence.

Hedonic Theory

John Dewey (1925) took this view to task and argued that such an inference contradicts reality in which "the organism is in a constant state of action" and that "activity indeed (is) the very essence of life." Dewey proposed that the drive for activity and stimulation sufficiently accounts for why children play.

In his theorizing on the motivation of play, Dewey came close to the thinking of modern theorists. In fact, he might be considered the bridge between the old school of philosophers and contemporary research oriented theorists. By proposing a reciprocal relationship between the stimulus and the subsequent response, Dewey tried to explain those circular and repetitive activities that occur so frequently in children's play. Dewey stated, "As stimuli direct this activity in one way or another, some of its modes are peculiarly rewarding. The stimulus not only arouses a certain kind of activity, but the responsive activity returns upon the stimulus so as to maintain it and to vary it. These variations supply the stimuli for keeping up more action." In this sense playful activity can be both rewarding and directing.

In order to maintain activity, variation and new stimulus-response relationships are necessary. The pleasure derived from participation in playful activity becomes the incentive for further activity. Dewey conjectured, "In like fashion, a baby plays with certain stimuli so as to keep up, with certain variations, a certain mode of action. Seeing a thing in a certain way evokes responses that make further seeings enjoyable." "Joy" in itself can be an incentive for further joy eliciting responses. Here is an obvious link with hedonic theory, which asserts that individuals behave to maximize their pleasure.

Traces of classical hedonic theory are present in most of the writings on play behavior. In the search for the ultimate motives directing play behavior one cannot disregard the importance of hedonic variables, a point on which most play theorists fully agree. However, there still exists considerable disagreement as to the weight to be attributed to hedonic variables, and whether positive affect or "joy" is the outcome rather than the motive that propels the individual into play behavior.

Karl Groos (1898) defined "joy in being a cause" as a viable motive for play. Also Freud (1928) stressed that many behaviors of the child, including play, are motivated by the "pleasure principle". He claims that free exercise of muscular activity occurring in most play activity constitutes a source of considerable pleasure and becomes the incentive for further participation. A different approach was advanced by Karl Buehler (1919) and Charlotte Buehler (1928) who proposed "functional pleasure" as a motive for play. They conceived of play as an activity initiated by a desire for functional pleasure and carried on as long as it affords pleasure. In similar vein, Rainwater (1922) viewed play as a noninstrumental and intrinsically rewarding activity, as "a mode of behavior . . . involving pleasurable activity of any kind, not undertaken for the sake of a reward beyond itself." In other words, the child plays because of the gratification that results from being engrossed in playful activity.

Related to the notion of "functional pleasure" is Duncker's (1940/41) version of "dynamic joys". Duncker, a philosopher, in elaborating on hedonic theory, identified "dynamic joys" as those experiences that derive from "the tensions, excitements, thrills, and reliefs of acting and resting." He offered the following examples of "dynamic joys": "the delight of driving at high speed, of fishing and hunting, of playing games, of following a plot (e.g., in reading a good detective story), etc."

Other hedonic theorists see play behavior as an activity "enjoyed for purely its own sake" (Tinklepaugh, 1942), or an activity which "expresses a joy of living," or "manifests a general exuberance" (Pycraft, 1912). Others conjecture that play flows from the pleasure of being active (Haigis, 1941), or that play merely results from "the active processes in which life manifests itself" (Dewey, 1925). These statements are so all-encompassing that it becomes virtually impossible to test their validity.

Hedonic theory was subjected to significant changes during the 1930's and 1940's as Cannon's (1932) views concerning homeostatic mechanisms, Skinner's (1938) innovations on operant conditioning with its major emphasis on reinforcement contingencies, and Hull's (1943) version of drive-reduction theory started to spawn research.

Homeostasis asserts that organisms strive to maintain steady or balanced biological or physiological states in order to safeguard their integrity and that this striving determines the bulk of behaviors emitted. Allen (1930), a hedonic theorist, challenged the universality of homeostatic based theory and its bold claim to account for the motivation of all behavior. He posed that pleasure is derived from many sensory experiences that are not related to the satisfaction of biologically or physiologically determined needs, and postulated a "craving for stimulation" to exist in sensory receptors. He further suggested that colors, odors, and sounds which are not bound up with any of the homeostatic states as defined by Cannon (1930) might elicit pleasant responses because they satisfy the craving for stimulation via the optical, olfactory, and acoustical receptors. Allen (1930) finally proposed that the satisfaction of the individual's desire for stimulation results in pleasure. With this observation, Allen had edged to the brink of contemporary theory on play behavior by making the critical leap that links the individual's "craving for stimulation" to play behavior.

To conclude, hedonic theory proposes that play is motivated and directed by a desire for pleasure and positive affect. "Joy" serves as an incentive. The conclusion follows simply: children indulge in play because of the joy that derives from play. It is true that play behavior yields positive hedonic experiences, but to assert that the child plays *only* to maximize or optimize the gratification or joy that derives from play does not interpret or explain anything; it does not furnish enough information to allow sound predictions; it is too simple an explanation for a very complex behavioral phenomenon (Beach, 1945).

It is customary to state that play behavior is "spontaneous activity" because that which sets it off cannot be seen. Lack of knowledge about the motivation of play usually leads to the simplistic hedonistic explanation: people play because they like to play. A more productive explanation would be to search for the causes of liking; the mechanisms behind the hedonic experience which we label "liking," "positive affect," "joy," or "pleasure."

Contemporary Play Theory

Precursors of stimulus-seeking explanations for play can be found as early as the eighteenth century. The contributions of a few German philosophers need mentioning. GutsMuths (1802) conjectured that boredom leads to a natural drive for play and activity. In essence he suggested that one of the goals of play is the pleasure that derives from activity by escaping the aversive effects of boredom and quiescence. This notion was based on the assumption that inactivity or quiescence is an aversive state of being which is avoided through participation in play.

underlies a huge variety of behaviors. Hebb (1955) agrees and stated that "living things by their nature are active" and have "a tendency to seek varied stimulation."

Humans when in a state of stimulus deprivation tend to seek varied stimulation and, when exposed to an overload of stimulation, tend to avoid it. This fact has led theorists to postulate the existence of an optimal range of stimulation or arousal as the preferred state of activation. They also state that by avoiding the extremes individuals will strive to approach such a state.

With roots in Helson's (1947, 1948) "adaptation level" theory, Leuba (1955, 1961) advanced the concept of optimal arousal, implying that humans behave to optimize their level of total stimulation or arousal:

> The organism tends to acquire those reactions which, when overall stimulation is low, are accompanied by increasing stimulation; and when overall stimulation is high, those which are accompanied by decreasing stimulation (Leuba, 1955).

The notion of optimal arousal assumes a principle of dynamic behavioral homeostasis, a tendency to maintain or restore the flow of sensory variation within an optimal range. The individual continuously strives to approach the state of optimal sensory variation because it is a rewarding state of activation and being. The state of optimal arousal does not imply behavioral quiescence; on the contrary, it implies a striving for activity and stimulus variation (Schultz, 1965) which suggests that activity is intrinsic in living organisms (Hunt, 1960).

The optimal range of arousal, a dynamic and varying state of activation, lies somewhere between two extremes on a stimulation continuum that extends from a state of extreme behavioral quiescence to a waking state of intense excitement or activation. According to Leuba (1955) the optimal range has to be defined in relative rather than absolute terms suggesting that it fluctuates over time and across individuals. It is influenced by the individual's internal state, stimulation history, and adaptation level to various intensities and kinds of stimulation, as well as the sensory input from immediately preceding environmental encounters.

Viewing optimal arousal slightly differently, Berlyne (1960) noted that "for an individual organism at a particular time, there will be an optimal influx or arousal potential. Arousal potential that deviates in either an upward or downward direction from this optimum will be drive inducing or aversive. The organism will strive to keep arousal potential near its optimum, which will normally be some distance from both the upper and lower extreme." Through experience individuals seem to have acquired mechanisms which predispose them to approach sources of moderate stimulation and withdraw from sources of intense stimulation (Schneirla, 1959), a finding that was interpreted as favoring the position of optimal arousal.

Related to drive theory and based on Cannon's (1930) notion of homeostasis, Schultz (1965) postulated another homeostatic mechanism, sensorista-sis, and defined it as a "drive for cortical arousal which impels the organism (in a waking state) to strive to maintain an optimal level of sensory varia-tion . . . a balance in stimulus variation to the cortex mediated by the ascend-ing reticular activation system." By implication Schultz stressed that the optimal state of arousal or activation accommodates a striving for activity and variation in stimulus input. Hunt (1969) also noted that individuals have a preference for an optimum amount of stimulus variation: a certain degree of incongruity is appealing, too little becomes boring and unappealing, while too much incongruity leads to conflict and avoidance behavior.

Literature on sensory deprivation and vigilance provides ample evidence postulating a predisposition to seek optimum arousal. Cofer and Appley (1964) reviewed the literature and finally concluded that stimulation is a state which organisms seek and which will reward them. A drive for optimal arousal is postulated which asserts that when alert, when the biological integrity of the individual (hunger, thirst, rest, security, etc.) is safeguarded, and when deprived of varying and information bearing sensory and cognitive experiences, humans will tend to generate or seek stimulation in order to achieve a state of optimal arousal. When optimally aroused, humans will try to maintain it.

Evidence exists suggesting that humans show a desire for behaviors associated with moderate uncertainty or incongruity. How to find the most preferred state of uncertainty is what Hunt (1961) called "the problem of the match." Hebb (1949), a leading promoter of the idea that individuals prefer a moderate state of uncertainty, postulated that a moderate discrep-ancy between what is predicted and what occurs may be pleasurable, whereas discrepancies beyond this amount may be unpleasant. Supportingly, Berlyne (1960) suggested that a repetitive correspondence between predictions and events leads to boredom, unpleasant affect and eventually heightened arousal. Maddi (1961) reported results indicating that in situations where rewards and punishments are at a minimum, both greatly unexpected and completely expected situations arouse negative affect, while moderately unexpected situations arouse positive affect. Also Helson (1948, 1959) has indicated that small deviations from the adaptation level regardless of the direction, contain positive hedonic value.

Arousal Seeking

The individual's need for intermediate uncertainty is generally interpreted as reflecting a desire for optimal information input and hence optimal arousal. Thus, arousal theory and hedonic theory are closely inter-twined. The proposed predisposition for an optimal influx of arousal potential is rooted in hedonic theory which predicts that aversive states are avoided and pleasant states are generally sought. Hedonic theory further asserts that the occurrence of a large population of behaviors, including play, relates to affective processes such that negative or aversive affect accompanying states of punishment, distress, anxiety and boredom are avoided, and positive affect such as reward, delight, joy and optimal stimulation are sought (Young, 1955; Brown, 1966; McClelland, Atkinson, Clark, and Lowell, 1966).

The tendency to seek stimulation of a certain individually preferred intensity can also be explained from the viewpoint of hedonic theory. The mere fact that the approximation to or continuation of an optimal influx of information is experienced as rewarding or reinforcing, reflects the fundamental role played by hedonic processes in determining preference. This is in effect the notion that is captured by the well-known "law of effect" advanced by Thorndike. This simple law predicts that individuals strive to reduce, remove or avoid distress or aversiveness. Behaviors that bring relief are likely to be learned.

The link between hedonic theory and arousal theory was also accepted by Mowrer (1960). He tied it to drive-reduction theory and reinterpreted sensory reinforcement effects in terms of the reduction of an aversive state or drive. Monotony and overstimulation were viewed as containing aversive attributes resulting in behaviors that avoid such states. The reduction of aversive states such as over-stimulation, according to Mowrer, should have reinforcing value.

Similarly, Schultz (1965) and Fowler (1967) proposed that familiar and constant stimuli contain tedium and boredom inducing qualities and that reinforcing properties are attributed to stimulus variation and change. In support, Jones and McGill (1967) found evidence suggesting that periods of information deprivation induce a drive process which motivates responses to stimuli of higher information value; conversely, periods of sensory overload elicit a preference for stimuli of lower information value.

In this sense, then, those behaviors having optimal arousal potential, which by definition is associated with positive hedonic value, will have a higher likelihood of recurring than those leading to an aversive state of under or over-arousal. Those behaviors become learned and readily incorporated in the individual's repertory of behaviors (Leuba, 1961). Play constitutes such a class of behaviors.

Sources of Arousal

To control the level of information, and via the flow of information its state of arousal, the individual depends on internal and external sources of stimuli. The stimuli from the external environment impinge upon the individual's somatic, visual, auditory, olfactory and visceral receptors which feed the impulses into (the reticular system of) the brain. The responses by the individual itself, as a result of cognitive and motor activity, provide the internal source of information. A closer investigation of these sources is necessary.

Not all external stimuli spontaneously appeal to the individual. Attending to stimuli from these major sources depends on preferences which in their turn are determined by the collative properties of the stimuli; i.e., their novelty, variation, complexity, conflict, uncertainty, and surprisingness (Berlyne, 1960). Fiske and Maddi (1961) simplified this list by proposing the term "impact", to express, collectively, the quantity of information a stimulus configuration contains.

Information can be defined as that which reduces uncertainty. Uncertainty derives from the respondent's inability to predict an outcome accurately when antecedent conditions are given. It is this information potential that determines the appeal a stimulus or a configuration of stimuli may have for an individual. Both Berlyne (1960, 1966) and Fiske and Maddi (1961) provide substantial evidence that the "impact" of the stimulus relates to arousal processes and to the initiation and maintenance of behaviors such as exploration, manipulation, and eventually play. If this relationship holds over a variety of behavioral settings, including play settings, then it becomes possible to manipulate the individual's state of arousal and ultimately his behavior by merely manipulating the informational input into the individual. This is a critical assumption.

A multitude of human behaviors are intrinsically motivated and have their origins in the dynamics of cognitive information processing within the brain. Berlyne (1960) identified these symbolic manipulations as "epistemic behavior" and suggested that novel, surprising, incongruous, dissonant, and complex combinations of cognitive experiences carry the potential to arouse the individual.

Epistemic behavior also relates to play. Ellis (1973) suggested that epistemic behavior is the core of play behavior, even in those situations where play is overtly dominated by motor activity. Fantasy play, game play, role play, imitative play, mere repetitive play, testing, construction, manipulation (Sutton-Smith, 1972) are all variations in play behavior that have roots in the dynamics of cognition and information processing. Theoretically they are instrumental in generating information flow through the individual and ultimately in arousing the individual. When stimuli become totally familiar and predictable, thus carrying very limited information for the individual, these sources of information will be ignored and alternatives will be sought.

Repetitious Responding

The theoretical formulation outlined above readily accounts for the presence of new and more complex forms in play. However, it has more difficulty in accounting for repetitious responding which is obviously also part of play. Each repetitious response should contain less information than its immediate antecedent, and its further repetition should eventually cease to be interesting. Why then are responses repeated? The remainder of this chapter tries to provide various answers. At times the individual emits activity that is apparently not guided by any reward other than that inherent in emitting the activity itself. The problem of explaining why mice run repeatedly in their wheels and why children repeat games endlessly required the postulation of a need for activity.

Research has shown that in many instances overt physical activity is instrumental in satisfying such needs as hunger, thirst, sex, or the escape from noxious or threatening stimuli. Kleitman (1963) and Cofer and Appley (1964) reported a number of studies indicating that increased overt activity or repetitive behavior relates to these basic needs. However, when these needs are satisfied, activity still prevails which suggests that physical activity does not relate solely to basic needs and their reduction or satisfaction. The fact that activity in itself has the potential to generate stimulation may account for the reason why physical activity is pursued "merely for the sake of being active."

The phenomenon of "spontaneous activity" is so prevalent that a drive for activity, independent from other drives, has been postulated. Cofer and Appley (1964) reviewed the relevant literature and conclude that the evidence available corresponded with the notion of an activity drive or drives. Nevertheless, they were reluctant to propose an explanation as to why such a drive exists. Lore (1968), on the contrary, concluded that there is remarkably little evidence that would justify the postulation of an autonomous activity drive and that it was best to look for other explanations for apparently motiveless behavior. The addition of a new drive to control behavior that did not fit neatly into another system is reminiscent of the instinct naming of yore. To go beyond merely adding a drive, it is necessary to propose a mechanism to explain the behavior.

It has been shown that the quiescence of sleep can be avoided by emitting motor responses. The processes involved in organizing and executing motor responses prevent the onset of sleep (Kleitman, 1963). Motor responding also prevents performance decrement during vigils (Mackworth, 1970). In both cases activity seems to prevent deactivation of the central nervous system by involving it in traffic with the periphery and beyond.

Since these observations, two attempts to explain repeated responses in terms of information or arousal seeking have been advanced. These notions assume that there are rewards and punishments inherent in the receipt of information that can be invoked to explain repetitious behavior. For this formulation to explain repetitious responding, it has to be shown that the repeated responses contain information that shifts arousal toward the preferred level.

The first explanation is relatively simple. It was invoked to explain the stereotyped behavior of retardates and caged animals (Ellis, 1973b). It postulates that even highly stylized and stable responses like body-rocking and cage-pacing contain some information. Since the responses are highly stable in time and space (Sprague, Werry, and Davis, 1969), random and systematic errors must be nulled so that the response remains constant. The nulling process necessarily involves feedback through which information necessary for detecting discrepancies is fed. Thus, a series of stable repeated responses necessarily produces a low level of information. These responses appear most often in chronically perceptually deprived individuals, and are emitted only when all alternate sources of information have been exhausted. These responses drop out if richer sources of information are allowed to compete for the attention of the individual.

In the second explanation, Berlyne (1960) attempts to explain the same stereotyped responses. He derived a two-stage explanation that argued that highly redundant responses are preferred under conditions of chronic perceptual deprivation. He claims that stress generates supra-optimal arousal, and that the emission of repetitious responses allows the individual to attend to highly redundant feedback. Since the higher brain functions as a single channel mechanism, attention to redundant responses displaces attention from high information bearing stimuli and thus reduces arousal. Redundant responding is a strategy for handling situations that are too arousing. Because repetitious responses are also emitted in situations where the information load is very low, Berlyne (1960) adds a second postulate. Boredom is such an aversive state that it induces anxiety. Once deprivation continues for a long enough period of time, individuals find themselves under stress and emit repeated responses to reduce their anxiety. This speculation involves a paradoxical effect. Highly redundant responses are instrumental in dealing with boredom. However, we shall return to these problems with some data in Chapter 6.

So far, only the undesirable repetitions born of boredom or stress have been dealt with. However, these are two categories of repetitious behavior that are adaptive and appear in the normal environment. In the first case repeated responding can be maintained by attaching consequences to the repetition. If repetitions are rewarded adequately, the aversive side-effects of redundancy can be overcome, and the individual will continue to emit the responses, i.e. the individual works. When all repetitious behaviors for which there is an extrinsic reward are eliminated, there remain those that seem to have an intrinsic reward.

The intrinsic rewards for these responses, it can be argued, lie in the information being processed. To answer questions about probabilistic events requires repetitious behaviors. Thus acquiring knowledge about which outcome is likely requires the same strategies from individuals as from the processes of science. To establish lawful relations among, or to be able to predict, probabilititistic outcomes requires the summation of the results of many responses. At the individual level, for example: determining whether a ball bounces true requires repeated bounces. Testing whether one can still perform a response, requires a further response. Acquiring a capacity to perform a response, i.e., to learn, requires the mapping of all the possibilities. In other words, in some cases it is not an individual response that answers the question but a series of repeated responses.

Summary

It seems that information-seeking theories of behavior have within them the potential to explain why new responses occur and why old responses reappear and under what circumstances. Attempts to test these formulations began about 1968 in the laboratory. The remainder of this monograph deals with these studies and other especially relevant work.

Chapter 3 / Attributes Modulating Preference

Introduction

The play of children is strongly shaped and directed by the environment. The environment can be defined as the ambient conditions together with the objects and persons present. A play environment or setting offers options from which a child is free to choose; options which may be preferred or rejected. From the act of choosing it can be inferred that at the moment children choose a particular interaction, they prefer it to the other available options. This chapter is built on these inferences and describes research that identified and manipulated some of the attributes modulating preference for interactions with objects or persons in a playful setting.

At the outset the emphasis will fall on a brief treatment of some studies dealing with the physical properties of objects and their effect on preference. The emphasis will then shift to a more elaborate treatment of the properties of objects, such as novelty, familiarity, and complexity, which Berlyne (1960) calls the collative properties. Finally, the empirical findings will be interpreted and explained using the information-seeking model.

Physical Properties

The studies described in this section were of an exploratory and practical nature. Simple physical properties of a set of play objects were varied and the effects on play activity observed. These attributes, independent of the subjects, were color, position in the room, degree of cover or encapsulation, and height. They all stemmed from a perceived pressure to find solutions to design problems that were besetting those concerned with providing toys and play environments for children. There was little theory guiding this work, and its original intent was to provide a catalog of attributes and the effects of manipulating them. However, it soon became obvious that the crucial variables modulating preference were not physical, and after a short while the focus of the work shifted. Nevertheless, the results of these preliminary studies are worth reporting.

Color

Color is an attribute considered important in determining preferences in play situations. In shops, in advertisements, on television, in parks, and in contrived play settings colors are selected to catch the eye and to promote the sale and usage of playthings. But is color really important in determining the selection and usage of play objects? Only a handful of studies have investigated this question. For example, Strain (1968) investigated children's preferences for color complexity and found that the more complex the color configuration, the more it was preferred. Does this finding also apply to play behavior?

Gramza and Witt (1969) and Solomon (1970) studied this problem in our laboratory. They allowed 35 nursery school children to play with blocks colored red, blue, green, and grey. These were presented in varied spatial arrays. In general, no significant preference for any one of the four colors occurred. Color preference was considered an insignificant factor in the block play of young children. There were positional preferences, however. The subjects clearly preferred block piles at either end of the semicircular array presented to them, regardless of the colors of the blocks in these positions. According to the authors, the impact of color as a determinant of preference appears to be fluid and dependent on the context. Therefore, color preferences executed in an abstract setting, for example, on paper or by verbal responses, may not necessarily predict usage of colored play objects in a more flexible, naturalistic play situation. As later suggested by Gramza (1973), great care needs to be taken in making extrapolations from certain types of laboratory studies (in this case, color preference research) to the more complex and open situations in which children ordinarily play.

Gramza, Witt, Linford, and Jeanrenaud (1969) repeated the color-preference study with Down's Syndrome children. Here again, no significant indications of preference for any one color were detected, and the Mongoloid children also showed no position preferences.

In both experiments all the blocks were the same shape. Color, the only variable, had no effect on the patterns of preference.

In another study conducted in the laboratory by Gramza and Scholtz (1974), the influence of visual complexity as a possible determinant of choice was investigated. Two colors, red and blue, in different patterns were presented on four cubical boxes, each $30'' \times 30'' \times 30''$ (see Fig. 3.1). The other attributes of the boxes were kept constant, and only visual complexity was varied. Sixty-eight nursery school children, 34 boys and 34 girls, were exposed to the wooden play boxes, two of which had sides patterned with a "simple" design, while the other two boxes were patterned with a "complex" design. Five 10-minute sessions on five consecutive days composed the total time of exposure. Each box had small 6-inch stepping blocks fixed to its sides to help the children climb. The boxes were placed in a square within the playroom, equidistant from each other and from the walls of the playroom. The positions of all boxes were rotated across sessions to balance for positional preferences. Individual preferences for the boxes were determined in terms of overt interaction or noninteraction with the test boxes; interaction was defined as occurring when any portion of a child's body extended onto a box. The results indicated no reliable preferences for either level of visual complexity in the children's use of the boxes. Only a slight preference for the complex patterned boxes was observed. The usage of all four boxes was highest on the first day of exposure and decreased significantly toward the fifth day, suggesting that degree of novelty was the important factor influencing interaction.

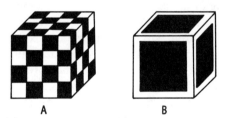

A   B

Fig. 3.1:   Complex and simple patterned boxes used in the visual complexity preference study. Here black corresponds to blue, white indicates red.

Functional Complexity

In free play encounters, the complexity of play objects has to be evaluated in terms of number, variety, and quality of responses the objects are capable of eliciting and sustaining. This is defined as the object's functional complexity. Functional complexity is an object's potential for play from the child's point of view. Although the boxes in the Gramza and Scholtz (1974) study differed in regard to visual complexity, their functional complexity remained the same. Accepting the null hypothesis argues that the critical variable was not the color pattern and supports the notion that for the children the two sets of boxes were equally attractive.

Gramza (1975) later manipulated functional complexity. The manipulability of a play object was selected as one of the critical modalities defining functional complexity. It was predicted that preference for a given play object will vary as a function of its manipulability. In the experimental analysis, 80 nursery school children, in groups of 10, were exposed to a number of stable play objects as well as a manipulable nylon rope. On two successive days, the children encountered the rope in a rather stable position, its ends fastened onto two stationary play objects, that is, in a state of low manipulability. On the other two days, the rope was left on the trestle completely free; this was defined as a state of high manipulability. As predicted, rope usage increased as manipulative options became available.

This study suggested that functional complexity seems to be a more critical attribute than simple physical properties.

Position Preference

Contrived play settings accommodate a fairly high proportion of the play behaviors of nursery and other preschool children. Some schools provide specific time, space, and opportunities for play activities. Certain locations are reserved for specific play objects. But which are the positions most frequented by players? Witt and Gramza (1970) studied the position preferences of four groups of nursery school children. A large and small trestle were interchanged between center and corner positions in a series of play sessions. The trestle in the center position received more use than the trestle placed in the corner position. A clear preference for play objects located in the center of a play environment was demonstrated. Witt (1970) repeated this study, using children with Down's Syndrome, and found supporting results.

These results are of critical importance when preferences for play objects are to be studied. Ignoring position preferences may introduce unexpected bias into measurements and result in distorted observations. The mere position of a play object may determine preference for it, regardless of the unique attributes of the object.

Encapsulation and Preference

Those who allow themselves the joy of watching children at play will occasionally observe their interest in playing within enterable or encapsulating spaces such as cave-like holes, large boxes or barrels, cozy self-built homes, or other hiding spaces. How can these behaviors be explained? It is easy to label them as instincts, or phylogenetic dispositions. Behaviors like these are very seldom submitted to experimental investigation, but Gramza used our laboratory to do so (1973b).

The tactile and visual stimulus dimensions of encapsulating spaces were considered as probable attributes modulating preference for them. Preschool children were systematically exposed to enterable boxes made of transparent, translucent, and opaque plexiglass presented within the context of a play-room setting. It was found that children at play prefer encapsulating objects which offer visual cutoff and darkness to those providing tactile enclosure alone. Children preferred the opaque and translucent boxes to the transparent ones, and generally, the opaque boxes were chosen over the translucent ones.

Gramza concluded that the cover-seeking behavior of children at play appears to gratify primarily the visual sense and secondarily the tactile sense. Gramza offered a few plausible explanations: exploration of stimulus contrast and variation provided by encapsulated space; retreat into defensible space and the feeling of exclusivity; contextual associations like playing "house," fright games, and fantasy play. In his general observations, he found contextual association to be the most noticeable and pervasive reasons for this kind of play.

The last of this interesting series of studies explored preferences for enterable play boxes having different numbers of open sides to vary their accessibility (Gramza, 1970). Again, preschool children were studied in a controlled, but relatively free, laboratory setting. The children strongly favored those boxes having the least degree of openness and the greatest degree of encapsulation. According to Gramza, children at play have a predilection for entering objects such as tunnels, play tubes, domes, and boxes, all of which are structures enclosing a relatively small space in which the child can experience variable degrees of sensory discontinuity from the larger surrounding environment. Much more research is needed to dissect and explain the motivations and reinforcers of these kinds of behaviors.

Height Preferences

Children love to climb. Much play apparatus is designed to cater to the child's tendency to explore heights.

Experimental evidence on height preference among playing children is meager. Karlsson and Ellis (1972) used the play laboratory to investigate height preference among young children. They expected to find that when children were repeatedly exposed to play objects offering a variety of height options, they would increasingly strive to play at higher levels. The height (from the floor) to which nursery school children climbed over a series of five free play sessions was studied. The play setting contained stable boxes, trestles, and an unstable rope net to define a setting of increasing task complexity. The results, however, did not suggest that the children preferred increased height, either from one session to another, or within each apparatus type or over all apparatus types.

The assumption of Karlsson and Ellis was that increasing the height of the vantage point of the player would alter his perceptions of the environment, and that therefore there should be a tendency for the preferred height to which children climb to increase as they seek novel stimuli or sensations. With experience, the growing abilities of children to climb on different kinds of play apparatus should result in a preference for greater heights. The failure to find the expected increase in height preference may be attributed to the fact that children need time and practice to develop the ability and confidence to climb high. The lack of clear trends suggests that the five 15-minute sessions, relatively brief episodes in the growth of the children, in fact reflected a cross-sectional sample of play activity and not a longitudinal one, as was anticipated.

Conclusions Concerning Physical Properties

This series of studies generated by our laboratory resulted in some critical findings which should be considered in future laboratory research on children's play behavior. Effects due to position and encapsulation are two examples of these. If ignored, distortions in the relationships of the independent and dependent variables are highly probable, thus undermining the internal and external validity of the results. The value of these studies lies in their potential contribution to the refinement of research methodology and to the elimination of biases which may result from the arrangement of the physical environment. To generate viable theory, however, empirical findings should be embedded in a theoretical frame of reference that is comprised of functional and systematic relationships among variables. For this reason the above trend in research received only limited attention in our laboratory. The emphasis shifted toward research on the collative properties of the stimuli themselves, i.e., their novelty, familiarity, and complexity.

Novelty and Familiarity

The research literature reflects two opposing views of the hypothesized preference for novelty. One group, supporting the early findings reported by Hebb (1949) and Berlyne (1950), furnished data in support of a preference for novelty; the other group, in agreement with the notion propagated by Zajonc (1968), asserted preference is a function of familiarity. These two views will receive extensive attention in the following pages.

Novelty

Attributes like change, variation, surprisingness, uncertainty, incongruity, and unexpectedness are usually associated with novelty. Novelty relates to previous encounters with stimuli and resides within the individual's informational interaction with the environment and its attributes. Individuals in varying degrees remember what has been encountered before. This enables them to compare present perceptions with information stored from previous experiences. Such information will determine to what extent the encountered experience is novel or familiar and depends on perceptual patterns stored in the brain which have to be decoded before the individual can identify novelty (Hebb, 1946). The discrepancy or incongruity between what is presently being perceived and what can be remembered from previous experiences determines the degree of novelty. Thus, novelty lies in the mind of the perceiver.

The degree of novelty which is attractive and preferred appears to present an optimal discrepancy between the informational input of the moment and the information already stored in the memory from previous encounters with similar situations (Hunt, 1966). Hebb (1949) noted that individuals tend to be preoccupied with "what is new but not too new" in any situation. When a novel experience is perceived as "too new" or too incongruous with previous encounters, avoidance behavior may occur. An optimal incongruity seems to be preferred (Hunt, 1961). The optimal degree of novelty varies with each individual's past experiences, expectations, and stage of development.

Fear of Novelty

Research evidence from a large number of species supports the fear-of-novelty hypothesis. Stimuli that are sufficiently incongruent with past experiences evoke fear and avoidance behavior while stimuli of moderate incongruity produce exploration (Hebb, 1946, 1949). When chimpanzees were presented with extraordinarily incongruent stimuli, strong fear responses were displayed (Hebb, 1966). Among primates, the younger animals tend to be more reluctant and slower in approaching strange persons than the older ones (Hebb and Riesen, 1943). Hinde (1974) reported that when young chimps become familiar with their environment, novel and strange objects elicit fear responses and avoidance behavior. In strange environments, familiar objects provide comfort which facilitates approach behavior.

Similarly, in human behavior the presence of an adult, like the mothering-one, usually ameliorates the fear-provoking effects of a strange and threatening environment. For example, Hutt (1966) noted that the latency of approach time toward a novel play object, by young children, was reliably shorter in the mere presence of a familiar adult than in a situation where an adult was absent. The latency of approach time to a novel play object is also determined by repeated exposure to the object.

In our laboratory this was verified by Jeanrenaud (1969). She found that it took 4- to 5-year-old children significantly longer to approach a novel play object in the first encounter than it took them to approach the same object in a second encounter the following day; there were no differences observed between boys and girls. The results were interpreted as supporting the theory of a strong approach-avoidance conflict in the first encounter with the novel play object. Latency of approach was influenced by the relative novelty of the play object. A perceived threat to the integrity of the child seems to initiate avoidance behavior.

Novelty and Preference

In environments where novelty is usually not associated with threat or fear, it has the power to attract the individual. In situations offering a choice between familiar and novel alternatives, both human infants (Ross, Rheingold, and Eckerman, 1972) and animals (Dember, 1961) tend to approach and interact with novel objects. In general, the evidence suggests that the presence of the mothering-one attenuates the fear and anxiety resulting from exposure to novel objects and facilitates an approach to them (Bronson, 1968). There is strong evidence that a small amount of novelty and variation is sought, especially in the presence of a familiar adult.

A large bulk of experimental data favors the notion that novel stimuli are a source of attraction. Since the early study on rats by Berlyne (1950), which indicated preference for associating with novel attributes of the environment, growing support for this theory has resulted from tightly controlled experimental studies on both animals and humans.

The tendency among human beings to seek out novel and varying stimulation was discussed in Chapter 2. It was pointed out by Buehler, as far back as 1930, that novel encounters with play stimuli seem to provide sensory feedback with positive hedonic value. Buehler claimed that children derive pleasure from engagements with play stimuli by looking at them, turning them over and feeling them, tapping them to produce sounds, and smelling them, thus investigating and testing the attributes of the play stimuli in various ways. Young children, while engaging in these kinds of novel encounters, are carried away by "functional pleasure," the joy of being active (Buehler, Hetzer, and Mabel 1928). A similar argument can be recognized in an observation by Hebb (1949), that a major source of pleasure resides in encountering something novel within the framework of the familiar.

There is much evidence demonstrating the tendency of children to seek out novel and varying stimulation. Cantor and Cantor (1964ab, 1966), for example, observed that when kindergarten-aged children were allowed to project both familiar and novel visual stimuli onto a screen, they projected the novel material for longer periods of time, most likely because of its richer information load. The magnitude of novelty-preference was inversely related to the amount of familiarization, thus supporting Welker's (1956abc) earlier findings on primates.

The early studies of M. W. Johnson (1935) and Cockrell (1935), and the later investiagtions by Mendel (1965) and Gilmore (1966ab) suggested a novelty-preference relationship in play situations. Mendel, in a study on young children, found that the preference value of a toy array increased as a result of its degree of novelty. Furthermore, older children, boys, and low-anxiety children preferred greater novelty more frequently than did younger children, girls, and high-anxiety children.

Some other studies tested preference patterns as related to visual stimuli. In attributing a tedium-producing property to familiar stimuli, Cantor (1968) found that fifth- and sixth- grade children showed a greater preference for novel visual stimuli, a finding that was confirmed by Cantor and Kubose (1969), and Siebold (1972).

From the data above it is clear that both animals and human beings tend to prefer novelty in visual as well as other stimuli. Even among infants this trend seems to hold. Stimuli with manipulative flexibility, which produce special effects, which have contrasting contours and texture, and contain many and variable elements were successful in commanding an infant's attention and devotion. Small discrepancies in degree of familiarity may influence the preferences of infants, even during the first months (Kagan, 1970). In addition, increased familiarity resulting from frequent encounters with stimulus configurations leads to variable attention; the infant favors stimulus configurations that resemble ones which have previously been encountered, but nevertheless differ from them to some extent.

The access to relatively novel stimulation in non-threatening settings seems to be rewarding. It has been argued that the increase in stimulation which results from encounters with novel and varying stimuli is mediated by by a rewarding state of physiological arousal (Ellis, 1973). The reward is strongly reinforcing, and, as early as 1930, Nissen pointed out that rats will suffer the pain of electric shock in order to achieve opportunity to explore an unfamiliar environment containing novel objects.

The few novelty studies conducted on nursery school children in our laboratory are worth mentioning here. One of these studies (Wuellner, 1969) was designed to investigate the effects of repeated exposure to initially novel play objects, or novel play objects introduced into a familiar environment. Wuellner searched for changes in the overt movement patterns of four- and five-year-old children over succeeding play sessions before and after introducing a novel play object. He used reduction of gross overt activity as the dependent variable to reflect preference for play objects. The playroom was equipped with a number of stationary items of play equipment, and the children were allowed to interact with them freely. After the first six sessions of 15 minutes each, a novel piece of play apparatus was introduced. The overall movement pattern was radically interrupted (see Figs. 3.2 and 3.3).

The early sessions of exposure to the relatively novel play objects elicited a high rate of activity which Wuellner explains in terms of abundant exploratory options available at that stage. The introduction of the novel play object

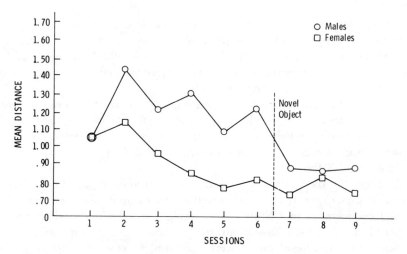

Fig. 3.2: Interaction effect of sex and sessions on the activity of young children. Note that in session 7 a novel object was introduced.

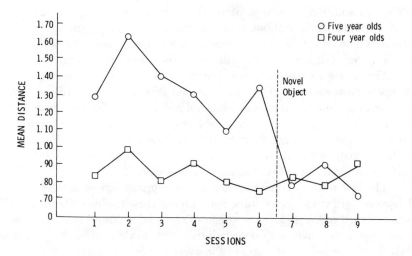

Fig. 3.3: Interactive effect of age and sessions on the activity of young children. Note that in session 7 a novel object was introduced.

later in the series exerted a powerful attraction. Wuellner stated: "Introduction of the novel object caused a significant decrease in activity in all other play areas. Since the novel object was new and required exploration, much time was spent investigating it." After its introduction a great reduction of the children's gross overt activity and movement was observed.

Wuellner presumably did not allow enough sessions after the introduction of the novel object to determine fully the effects of continued exposure to novelty. Nevertheless, the relatively strong preference for novelty that manifested itself is consistent with the novelty-preference literature in general.

The urge for novelty and variation does not always culminate in preferences for objects, however, but may also result in exploration involving different kinds of overt activity. In their gross overt activity children attempt to introduce novelty by varying the ways in which activity is expressed. They vary their location in space, they move faster and slower, they run, walk, stop, crawl, jump, sit, swing, hide, etc. Through overt activity children test their abilities and their effects and derive joy from it (see Sutton-Smith, 1971, 1972).

Approach to, and association with, a novel source of stimuli most likely reflects a positive hedonic value in the source, and withdrawal a negative hedonic value (Hunt, 1969). Attraction is either induced or terminated because it is associated with positive or negative affect. Hedonic mechanisms, despite the reluctance of scientists to integrate them into explanations and predictions of behavior, still remain a dominant undertone of reinforcement models of behavior. Hedonic mechanisms seem to account for the individual's attraction to novelty.

Familiarity and Preference

The evidence reviewed above suggests that moderately novel stimuli are initially preferred, but that preference declines as a result of familiarity through exposure. Zajonc (1968), however, hypothesized a linear relationship between mere repeated exposure and liking, with preference and attraction increasing with familiarity. Zajonc's hypothesis was rooted in evidence from a large number of correlational studies involving the frequency of everyday words and their evaluative meaning, and a series of studies involving the effect of repeated exposure to different stimuli and preference for them.

A change in preference and liking of a stimulus which results from frequency of exposure was presumed to reflect the attitude toward the stimulus. Preference was determined from evaluative verbal responses or by inference from individual interactions with the stimuli in question. Thus, a high affective rating or repeated interaction with stimuli was accepted as an indication of preference for those stimuli.

The Zajonc familiarity-preference hypothesis has received some experimental support. Evidence shows that repeated exposure to initially adverse stimuli leads to diminished dislike with exposure (Perlman and Oskamp, 1971; Brickman *et al.*, 1972; Saegert, Swap, and Zajonc, 1973). A number of other studies supported the predicted enhancement in attractiveness of a stimulus with increasing frequency of exposure (Zajonc and Rajecki, 1969; Harrison, 1968a, 1969; Harrison and Zajonc, 1970; Schick, McGlynn, and

Woolam, 1972). Only rarely were attempts made to explain why this relationship exists.

An explanation for the proposed familiarity-attraction tendency was proposed by Harrison (1968b). Exposure to novel stimuli should elicit a tension state (response competition) with aversive side effects and subsequent negative attitudinal ratings; reduction in response competition as a result of repeated encounters should lead to positive affect and attitudinal ratings. More recently the Zajonc hypothesis has received further support (Harrison and Zajonc, 1970; Matlin, 1970, 1971; Harrison and Hines, 1970; Harrison, Tutone, and McFadgen, 1971; Zajonc, Swap, Harrison, and Roberts, 1971). But despite all this evidence, substantial controversy still exists concerning the familiarity-preference relationship.

Maddi (1968) noted that with repeated exposure, familiarity shades over into monotony, with the attendant negative affect and subsequent attitudinal ratings. Three recent studies supported the presumed positive relationship between novelty and hedonic value (Cantor, 1969; Berlyne, 1970; Siebold, 1972). The Zajonc hypothesis seems to be based on the premise that unfamiliarity mediates mild conflict and discomfort resulting in negative affect toward the novel stimuli encountered. When this notion was applied to stimuli from objects other than human beings in studies of preference for novel versus familiar stimuli, it received strong contradiction. For instance, many studies conducted on children found a preference for novel stimuli over familiar ones (Cantor, 1963; Odom, 1964; Harris, 1965; Gullickson, 1966; Endsley, 1967). Cantor (1968), after asking children to state their preferences, in addition to observing their overt behavioral preferences for visual stimuli, summarized the results: "Fairly clear evidence for preference on the part of fifth- and sixth-grade children for nonfamiliarized as opposed to previously familiarized visual stimuli" was found.

It is clear by now that the novelty-preference and familiarity-preference controversy has not been resolved although the evidence leans toward a theory favoring a general novelty-preference disposition.

In a later discussion we will return to this novelty-attraction and familiarity-preference paradox. Apart from novelty or familiarity, preference is also mediated by other perceived qualities, such as stimulus complexity.

Stimulus Complexity

The complexity of a stimulus is another attribute which modulates responsiveness and preference. Berlyne (1960) notes that the complexity level of a stimulus (which can be an event, object, situation, etc.) can be increased or decreased by manipulating the number of distinguishable components and their dissimilarity, so that the elements cannot be categorized into just one item and reacted to simply. More simply, stimulus complexity refers to the amount of variety or diversity in a stimulus pattern (Cantor, 1963). This definition, proposed by Berlyne, is accepted as the comprehensive definition for our purposes.

Novel stimuli have the power to elicit responsiveness; complex stimuli, however, are able to sustain responsiveness. This fact was convincingly demonstrated by Welker (1956abc) in his now classical studies on the play behavior of primates. His experiments indicated that exposure to novel more complex objects generated more exploratory, manipulative, and playful responses than novel and simple objects. The more complex the play object, the slower the process of habituation. This was presumably due to the greater number and variety of novel stimuli embedded in complex configurations. Each stimulus had to become familiar before the total configuration was ignored as no longer appealing. Further studies on primate play (Harlow, Harlow, and Suomi, 1971; Suomi and Harlow, 1971; Russell and Pearce, 1971) generally echoed these results. The impact, or attractiveness of a configuration of stimuli, seems to vary with its complexity.

Among human subjects, complexity also sustains responsiveness (Munsinger and Weir, 1967; Dent and Simmel, 1968; Faw and Nunnally, 1968; Unikel and Harris, 1970; Arkes and Boykin, 1971; Leckart et al., 1972). The early playground studies by M. W. Johnson (1935) and Cockrell (1935) also furnish suggestive evidence on this point, although their manipulation of play apparatus complexity was actually unintentional. They found that complex apparatus settings sustain a greater variety of engagement with play objects than do simple ones.

Berlyne and his associates have repeatedly shown that individuals devote more time looking at complex patterns than simple ones. Furthermore, objects that offer more varied or more irregular stimulation attracted more vigorous and prolonged exploration (Berlyne, 1966), which again suggests the sustaining capacity of complexity.

Preference for stimuli does not solely depend on the mediation of collative properties such as novelty and complexity; experiences preceding exposure also have a modulating effect. Studies of response patterns to visual stimuli provide access to this problem. It was postulated that chronically deprived children would seek less rich stimulus situations which would provide a level of stimulation that they could tolerate. Hicks and Dockstader (1968) tested this hypothesis and found that a significantly greater number of deprived children showed a preference for less complex and novel stimuli than did those children who were not chronically deprived.

Deprivation immediately prior to stimulation has a different effect. Leckart et al. (1972) found that time spent exploring fairly complex polygons increased with the duration of prior perceptual deprivation. The length of time spent looking was a direct function of deprivation level and stimulus complexity. Similarly, Berlyne (1971) concluded that the strength of the tendency to seek exposure to relatively complex stimulus material varies inversely with the level of exteroceptive information processing just before the choice. In another study, Berlyne and Crozier (1971) found that the less visual stimulation received just before making a choice, the more inclined an individual will be to seek exposure to more complex patterns. Even a few seconds of stimulus deprivation is enough to increase the tendency to seek exposure to relatively complex stimuli. To account for their results, the authors suggested that more complex patterns provoke a greater amount of uncertainty and conflict, leading to an increase in curiosity and subsequent preference for exposure to them.

It is generally assumed that individuals grow more complex with age, each advance building on previous ones. Experiences and their variety combine and their effects accumulate in the memory. Thus, in general, older children should reveal preferences for greater stimulus complexity than younger children. Brennan, Ames, and Moore (1966) found this to be the case. Also, Black, Williams, and Brown (1971) found that preference for stimulus complexity tends to increase with age. Four-year-olds preferred the more complex stimuli and three-year-olds the less complex stimuli. However, some studies employing several age groups have shown that preference for certain complex or novel stimuli tends to decrease with age (Pielstick and Woodruff, 1964; Munsinger, Kessen, and Kessen, 1964; Baltes, Schmidt, and Boesch, 1968). How are these contradictory results to be explained? It is likely that older children, being more experienced with the stimuli perceived the experimental "complex" stimuli as simple. In such a case a relatively low preference is to be expected.

Although it can be accepted that preference for complexity is individually determined (Dember and Earl, 1957), due to the uniqueness of each individual's sensory and environmental history, there is good reason to accept the theory that individuals unfold in a pattern of preference for increasing complexity. Each advance depends on previous ones with the preferred level for complexity located slightly above the complexity level at which the individual is presently situated (Dember and Earl, 1957). When given the choice, individuals expose themselves to external stimuli offering a degree of complexity slightly exceeding their current level of complexity. Preference for complexity proceeds by gradually paced increments. Appropriately complex stimuli are therefore called "pacers" by Sackett (1965). As the individual's level of complexity rises to the pacer's level, a new, higher pacer is selected (Arkes and Boykin, 1971). Haber (1958, 1966) and McClelland and Clark (1966) identified the momentary level of complexity as the adaptation level (AL). The AL may vary over time, but the preferred level for complexity remains slightly above the AL at which the individual is presently situated (Unikel and Harris,

1970). Hence the preferred level of complexity functions like a "pacer" favoring interaction with progressively complexified stimuli.

Novelty, Complexity, and Play

As suggested by the Welker studies, novelty and complexity seem to function together to modulate play behavior. Due to the interactive nature of novelty and complexity, it becomes difficult to separate the effects of novelty from those of complexity. In general, novelty has been seen as a quality which elicits responsiveness and complexity as a quality which sustains it.

The studies of Berlyne (1960, 1969) postulate a relationship between play behavior and stimulus attributes such as novelty, complexity, incongruity, and variation. Experimental evidence supporting this hypothesis has emerged rather slowly. The studies from our laboratory are among a small number of experiments which directly bear on the relationship between complexity and play behavior.

Hutt's (1966) finding, that three- to five-year-old children spent a greater proportion of time manipulating a lever which made a bell or a buzzer sound than one which produced only visual feedback, can be interpreted in terms of a preferential interaction with complex play objects.

In our laboratory, Wade and Ellis (1971) analyzed the activity levels of eight boys and eight girls exposed to different levels of environmental complexity. A higher level of environmental complexity was generated by increasing the number and variety of play objects within the play setting and by increasing the size of the playing group (see Fig. 3.4). It was expected that the high-complexity environment would stimulate the players, causing them to become more active, relative to their activity level in the simple setting.

The subjects were allowed to play alone, in dyads and in quadrads, in the two environmental conditions of low and high functional complexity, for 60 minutes per session. These were the independent variables. The activity level of the children as expressed by their heart rates, as well as observation scores of gross overt activity were dependent variables.

In general, the data revealed that increasing the complexity of the stimulus environment by increasing group size raises the general activity level of the children. The more children there were in the setting, the more activity there was. The two physical environments of low and high complexity, however, failed to produce reliable differences in the activity levels of children, contrary to what was expected.

The impact of the social environment as a source of arousal and subsequent elicitor of activity was more powerful than that of the physical environment. This can be explained both by the social facilitation theory and by the

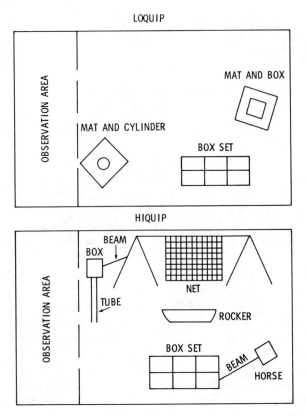

Fig. 3.4:   Schema showing the floor plans of the two levels of environmental
complexity used in the study of activity levels of children at play.
"LOQUIP" signifies "low complexity equipment", and "HIQUIP" the
opposite.

information seeking hypothesis. The information-seeking explanation claims
that social manipulation proved to be more effective because the interaction
with other children presented a panoply of changing stimuli, whereas the
high complexity physical environment, once explored and exploited failed
to provide interactions which were more complex than those of the simple
condition. Social facilitation theory states that the mere presence of others
constitutes a source of arousal leading to increased activity (Zajonc, 1965;
Martens, 1969, 1975; Cottrell, 1972). The fact remains that increases in social
complexity have an influence on the activity level of children in a play setting.

Other data from the same study, this time published by Wade, Ellis,
and Bohrer (1973), also produced relevant findings. It was assumed that the
interaction between arousal to action caused by environmental stimuli and
recovery from that activity should generate biorhythms in the activity levels

of the children. The data was submitted to spectral analysis to locate significant biorhythms. The methods and central findings are taken up again in more detail in Chapter 4. However, to summarize, there was a tendency toward 40-minute (slow frequency) and 15-minute (fast frequency) biorhythms. Again manipulating, the group size produced the strongest effects. In this case, the strongest biorhythms occurred when the children played in pairs. The differences generated by changes in the apparatus configurations were not significant.

Another study conducted in our laboratory searched for a relationship between environmental complexity and play behavior (Gramza, Corush, and Ellis, 1972). They exposed 40 four- to five-year-old preschool children to a simple and a complex play apparatus and determined their preferences. The children were introduced to a traditional and rather bare 92-inch-high climbing trestle (low-complexity apparatus), and to another one that was modified by the addition of two 48-inch-square blue chipboard panels, fastened one to each of the sloping sides of the trestle (high-complexity or complexified apparatus).

A reliable preference for complex play objects over simple ones was found. Also, exposure to moderately novel play objects leads to strong initial preference, but interaction with them decreases as a result of repeated exposure, the rate of decrease depending on the complexity of the apparatus. As play stimuli become more familiar as a result of repeated exposure and encounters, they lose their attraction, presumably because they are experienced as carrying only a modest amount of meaningful information. Complexity seemingly mediates the rate of familiarization as a result of mere repeated exposure.

The Familiarity-Preference Hypothesis Revisited

Attitudinal ratings of stimuli to which subjects have been repeatedly exposed are mediated by the complexity of the stimulus configuration. This hypothesis will be examined in the next pages. Extant research bearing on the problem, as well as a few related studies from our laboratory, will be reviewed.

One of the first studies of the mediation effects of stimulus complexity on subjects repeatedly exposed to the stimulus was reported by Saegert and Jellison (1970). Their results indicated that preference for a simple stimulus had at first increased, and then decreased markedly. Complex stimuli, however, continued to grow in preference with frequency of exposure, up to twenty-five 3-second exposures. These results were interpreted as supporting the Zajonc thesis. A word of caution seems justified, however. It is doubtful whether the trends over a hundred similar exposures would continue to uphold the Zajonc premise of increased preference with increased exposure.

Generally, evidence has shown that sustained responsiveness is a function of stimulus complexity. According to Berlyne (1970), preference for simple stimuli should decline faster than for complex stimuli. In a sequence of five experiments, Berlyne (1970) found results running counter to the Zajonc thesis. His results suggested that homogeneous sequences of stimuli declined in judged pleasantness more than sequences in which several different kinds of stimuli were interspersed, that simple stimuli became less pleasant as they became less novel, and that the pleasantness of complex stimuli declined less rapidly or even increased. Berlyne's hypothesis was substantiated. It predicted a decrease in the hedonic value of simpler patterns and an increase in the hedonic value of more complex patterns, as repetition reduces novelty. Let us consider the theoretical basis for these predictions.

Berlyne noted that preference for and liking of simple stimuli should decline faster as a result of repeated exposure, relative to complex stimuli. An integration of hedonic theory with arousal processes was formulated to explain this phenomenon. A state of high arousal is experienced as aversive, and behaviors that reduce high arousal will be rewarding and experienced as pleasant. A state of relatively low arousal, such as boredom, is unpleasant, and stimulus conditions that produce a moderate increase in arousal will be associated with positive hedonic value. Berlyne then suggested that positive hedonic value reaches a maximum with moderate arousal potential and then, as arousal potential increases further, hedonic value takes on lower and lower positive values and finally becomes negative.

Attributes like stimulus novelty and complexity are factors which affect arousal states. Novel stimuli of moderate complexity tend to propel the individual's state of arousal toward the optimum, with which positive hedonic value is associated. Familiar and simple stimuli induce a drop in arousal below the optimal range, which increasingly produces negative hedonic value. Berlyne pointed out that this conception of boredom explains why ratings of simple and familiar stimuli are sometimes negative. If the initial impact of a novel and complex stimulus pattern is very high, it may induce high arousal, and the uncertainty, conflict, and disorientation (see Berlyne, 1963) which result may produce negative affect.

Repeated exposure reduces the arousal potential of stimuli. When exposed to highly complex stimuli the individual will initially experience an aversive state of high arousal and will be apt to rate the stimuli as negative. As the stimuli become more familiar, subsequent reduction in arousal potential occurs, leading to a state of optimal arousal, a pleasant state. Finally, even initially complex stimuli lose their arousal potential as they become more familiar and predictable. Their positive hedonic value declines, and they become less preferred. From this it follows that attitudinal ratings of complex patterns will increase to a peak and will then fall off as a result of continued exposure.

Does the familiarity-preference hypothesis also bear on social stimuli? In 1950 Homans noted, "If the frequency of interaction between two or more persons increases, the degree of their liking for one another will increase." Sherif and Sherif (1953) allowed boys in novel groups to work and play together for a time in a summer camp and observed an increase in interaction and liking for one another. A later study duplicated these results (Sherif, White, and Harvey, 1955). Newcomb (1956) hypothesized that attraction varied inversely with interpersonal distance and directly with frequency of reinforcing or rewarding interactions over time. For the experiments conducted in our laboratory, the hypothesis that mere exposure could account for enhanced interpersonal attraction was accepted, and Newcomb's additions to this hypothesis were deemed unnecessary. Evidence for this has come from experiments where subjects were exposed to others indirectly—by photographs or by name (Zajonc, 1968; Harrison, 1969; Perlman and Oskamp, 1971)—but it can be argued that such experiments only provide suggestive evidence as they do not mirror the complexities of real interpersonal encounters. "Mere repeated exposure" usually involves reciprocal overt and covert forms of interaction, even when the persons concerned merely observe one another. Photographs or names are surrogates only. This objection was met by Saegert, Swap, and Zajonc (1973) who exposed subjects to interaction with each other and reported that "mere repeated exposure of people is a sufficient condition for enhancement of attraction, despite differences in favorability of context, and in the absence of any obvious rewards or punishments by these people."

The familiarity-liking relationship seems to be a well-documented hypothesis describing the interaction of human beings. Liking is dependent on exposure (see Lott and Lott, 1965), and independent of the conditions under which the exposure took place. But, in situations where exposure is associated with negative or positive contingencies, the familiarity-preference relationship may get distorted in one direction or another. In real life encounters it is extremely difficult to discriminate effects due to "mere repeated exposure" from effects due to positive or negative contingencies associated with exposure.

To summarize, there is controversy over whether the Zajonc hypothesis is valid for both objects and people. In general, studies that have dealt with exposure to social stimuli are fairly consistent in rendering support to the familiarity-preference hypothesis, while less congruity exists among studies utilizing nonsocial stimuli.

Attributes like novelty and complexity seem to interact in modulating preference for objects and peers. This problem became the subject of an experiment undertaken by the present authors. They studied the preference of children for objects or peers in a naturalistic setting which offered repeated opportunities to interact with both. The results delineated the effects due to novelty, complexity, and repeated exposure and were reported in two separate papers (Scholtz and Ellis, 1975ab).

Sixty 4- to 5-year-old children were exposed to one of three initially novel environmental conditions. One was of low complexity, another of high complexity (see Figs. 3.5 and 3.6), and a third was progressively complexified.

Fig. 3.5: Fisheye view of the simple environmental complexity setting used to manipulate preferences for objects and peers.

Operationally, the environment containing the greatest number and variety of play objects constituted the high-complexity setting; the low-complexity setting contained the fewest and least varied play objects. The complexified setting progressed from the low-complexity setting for the entire first week, to a setting of intermediate complexity for the second week, and finally to a high-complexity setting for the last week. The subjects were exposed to the same settings of low and high complexity for fifteen 15-minute sessions during three consecutive weeks. The complexified setting, however, was changed at the end of each week.

Fig. 3.6: Fisheye view of the complex environmental setting used to manipulate preference for objects and peers.

The two dependent variables were object preference and peer preference. Object preference was inferred from engagement or absence of engagement with play objects in the playroom. Peer preference occurred when a subject played with one or more peers when not engaged in playing with the play objects. This variable included activities such as chasing each other around, wrestling, and playing games in small groups in the open space away from the play objects. Playing with peers while in the open space was considered to be a gross measure of peer preference and was presumed to reflect the child's attitude toward them resulting from repeated exposure.

The results showed that the complex condition elicited far more object preference than the simple condition (Scholtz and Ellis, 1975a). Object preference declined sharply with familiarity, in contradiction to the Zajonc prediction.

Peer preference increased with repeated exposure (see Fig. 3.7). This trend developed in the low-complexity as well as the high-complexity setting. Differences in complexity of the setting did affect the patterns of peer preference. During the three weeks, exposure to the low-complexity environment resulted in reliably more play with peers than did exposure to the high-complexity environment.

Some important inferences are to be drawn from these results. On entering the low-complexity setting for the first time, the children preferred

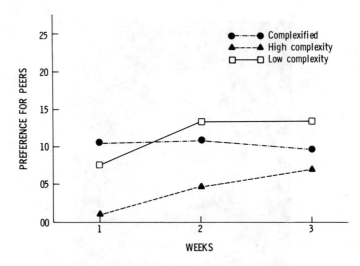

Fig. 3.7: Effects of environmental complexity and exposure on preference for interaction with peers.

interaction with the novel play objects to interaction with their peers. As exposure increased and the play stimuli became more familiar and predictable, their information appeal diminished. A group of peers, even familiar ones, is seemingly more complex and variable than a collection of familiar and unchanging play objects. With the increasing familiarity of the play objects, preference shifted to the more interesting peers.

This description must be slightly modified when applied to those children playing in the complex setting. There, the initial impact of the apparatus was enhanced by virtue of its considerable complexity. Because of the high variation in options the apparatus was capable of eliciting, it generated and sustained a high degree of engagement; it was much preferred. Sustained exposure did lessen the impact, however, and there was a clear trend toward increasing preference for peers over time, although the interest in play objects did not bottom out during the experiment, as it did in the low-complexity setting.

To summarize, Scholtz and Ellis noted that preference for interaction with peers increased as a result of repeated exposure, while preference for interaction with play objects decreased, with the rate of decrease being influenced by the complexity of the physical setting (see Fig. 3.8). The high-complexity setting sustained more interaction with play objects and less interaction with peers than the low-complexity setting. Contrary to Zajonc's prediction but in line with Berlyne's, repeated exposure to play objects diminishes preference for them, the rate in decline being determined by the complexity of the stimulus.

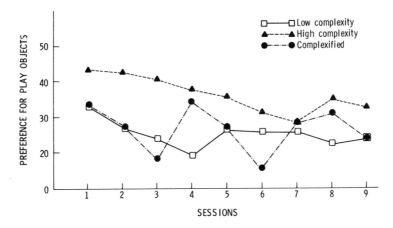

Fig. 3.8: Effect of repeated complexification on the preference for play objects.

The Zajonc hypothesis explains the peer preference data but does not account for the interaction between the nature of the stimulus sources (peer or object), and their familiarity and complexity. The earlier study by Gramza, Corush, and Ellis (1972) showed that the more complex the stimulus, or configuration of stimuli, even in play settings, the longer the time required for habituation, and the slower the rate of decrease in response. Similarly, in the study by the present authors the complex configuration of play apparatus elicited and sustained more interactions than did the simple setting. These results were interpreted in terms of the individual's appetite for information. It seems that as the information in one source, the apparatus, was exhausted, the children turned to the other available source, their peers. The authors finally concluded that the rapid reduction of uncertainties in the simple setting triggered an earlier switch of preference from objects toward engagements with peers.

The authors' second report (1975b) gives a more detailed analysis of response patterns during the first day of exposure to the play settings, as well as a discussion of preferences that were manifested in the complexified condition. During the first session, preference to interact with the novel objects peaked in all three conditions and then decreased steadily as a result of repeated exposure and familiarity. Responsiveness to the high-complexity setting was remarkably greater throughout the first session than was the case with the simple settings at that time. Throughout the entire experiment the high-complexity environment induced substantially more engagements than did the other two conditions (see Fig. 3.8).

In the complexified setting, the novelty and complexity of the apparatus were simultaneously manipulated. Increments in both novelty and complexity occurred at the beginning of the second and third weeks when novel play objects were added to the setting in order to escalate complexity. Highly reliable increases in preference for play objects occurred on each of these occasions. These results refute the familiarity-preference hypothesis.

Summary

This review of experiments undertaken by the authors and other researchers has indicated that attributes such as novelty, familiarity, and complexity can be fruitfully manipulated to modulate the play behavior of young children. In contrived as well as naturalistic environments, novel and variable play stimuli generally attract the attention and interaction of the child and give rise to exploratory and play behavior. Familiarity with play objects, however, has the potential to inhibit playful interaction with them. In the case of social stimuli, familiarity seems to promote interaction, attraction, and ultimately, social play.

Stimulus complexity, although difficult to quantify, seems to sustain behaviors which have been elicited by the novel components in a complex configuration. In general, the results of the research described here seem to support the thesis that novel and complex stimuli are sought because of their potential to convey information and activate the child.

It was proposed in the preceding chapter that individuals have a propensity to process information and that the play behavior of children is strongly modulated by this need. It was also noted that stimulus attributes of the external environment, of which novelty and complexity are examples, constitute a critical source of information upon which, it is presumed, the state of arousal is dependent.

Experimental evidence suggests that novelty, variation, and complexity are stimulus attributes with the potential to convey information and to modulate arousal. These attributes are also strong determinants of preference. Thus, by manipulating these attributes, it becomes possible to modulate a child's state of arousal and the play behavior which result.

Chapter 4 | Activity of Children

Introduction

Activity, a central area of concern in this monograph has not yet been defined. It means no more than the state of being active or that which connotes action. Activity also refers to the sum total of the actions or behaviors emitted by a subject. Clearly activity can refer to any class of actions, glandular, muscular, or electrical, that occur in the subject. However, here we use the word to refer to the propensity of a child to emit overt behaviors, and this refers primarily to behaviors using the skeletal muscle system.

Intentional Behavior

Overt behaviors are usually not reflexive but are adaptive in that they appear to be guided by some intent to cause an effect. The intention guiding another's act can only be inferred by the observer, and this process often irritates purists who wish to purge the behavioral sciences of such hypothetical constructs as intention or motive. However, adult observers have long histories of being rewarded for correctly inferring the intent of others' streams of behaviors, and are reliable users of the concept of intention to predict behaviors in others. Given that behavioral science is being conducted by humans, it seems to us to be best served by allowing the existence of "intention" as an organizing principle lying between a stimulus and response. Therefore, activity becomes a stream of purposive observable acts emitted by an individual presumably in response to events.

Behavior which seems to an observer to be organized by rewarding consequences is easy to understand. In fact, we say that the child is working for a reward or to avoid a punishment. However, quite often it is not possible to point out the reinforcing event, in which case the behavior is usually labelled as intrinsically reinforced behavior. This behavior is difficult to study since the consequences of the responses are not readily manipulable by an observer. These kinds of behaviors satisfy the definitions for play in that they are determined, not by readily observable consummatory acts, but seem to be sustained by the processes of acting itself. This process orientation is playful in that often highly variable responses, the kind of behaviors that are classically labelled error, predominate. The internal events reinforcing them were discussed in Chapter 2.

When the acts are clearly organized by the attachment of consequences to criterion responses we are in the habit of saying that the individual is working for a reward. When the acts are not tied to obvious external reinforcers the behavior is said to be intrinsically motivated and satisfies a common definition for play. Often these apparently surplus behaviors are defensively labelled as trivial and ignored, or subjected to negative reinforcers to bring the subject back on track towards a criterion response.

Unfortunately at any given time the sources of antecedent stimuli impinging on individuals as well as the intentions of the individuals vary and are often at variance with the expectations of the observer. So inferences of appropriateness and inappropriateness can be made both by the actor and observer. When these are in sympathy all is well, but when the actor and observer are at odds there is either conflict, one or other complies with the expectations of the other, or the behavior is ignored as irrelevant. In highly structured settings like classrooms and dining rooms, however, the apparently irrelevant or inappropriate behavior is not ignored, and efforts are made to change behavior. Failure to respond results in conflict, and the actor is labelled naughty or deviant.

So acts, or when considered collectively, activity, can be appropriate or inappropriate according to an observer's judgment. If the contingencies are set to reward certain behaviors and those behaviors are desired, then the activity is classified and dealt with as appropriate. When this is not so, it may be labelled maladaptive and the individual considered deviant.

Activity Level

The quantity, intensity, and nature of activity obviously varies with any child from time to time and from setting to setting. Furthermore, the average level of activity can also be presumed to vary from child to child. Thus the concept of intraindividual and interindividual variation in activity is an important one. A range of activity can be expected. Differences in activity level, a child's typical quantity of activity, are normal. It follows directly that one source of apparently deviant activity levels is the naturally occurring and desirable variation among children.

So activity can be play and/or work, appropriate and inappropriate, variable or consistent, but it is assumed to be determined in some way. Charting the determinants will enable those concerned to understand why and when people are active, and perhaps shed light on the recently discovered problem of hyperactivity.

Studying Activity

This chapter deals with some of the research which tried to disentangle factors that influenced the nature and quantity of gross motor activity emitted by the child in settings in which there was some freedom as to the kind and quantity of activity deemed appropriate by the child.

As a general principle, no observer or experimenter told the children what to do during the studies reported. The children were placed in environments and left to respond. However, the environments were in themselves sources of influence and these were systematically varied so that activity observed was the result of an interaction between the nature of children themselves at that time and the task demand characteristics of the activity setting. Thus the subtle guiding of children's behaviors by the presence of adults was usually avoided. Against this backdrop then, many studies of the nature and quantity of behavior emitted by children in the service of their own intentions were conducted.

Most observers would label the activity studied play. In the sense of the definitions of play dealt with here it usually was. The children were not working for externally applied consequences; there were no criterion behaviors. There was some freedom to emit a response from an array of potential responses. In that sense the behavior was playful. However, the behavior was not random, it followed complex themes and involved interaction with peers and with the environment. In a sense the struggle to explain activity was part of the same struggle to explain play. In fact, for a long time the subject matter of the laboratory's focus was often referred to as playful activity.

The first step necessary for the study of playful activity was the development of an unobtrusive system for its quantification. This was described in detail in Chapter 1. In investigating the capacity of the early fisheye system Wuellner (1969) conducted an experiment. He used the fisheye system to record the locomotor activity of young 4- and 5-year-old boys and girls, in a naturalistic setting—the Play Research Lab at the Children's Research Center. Repeated play sessions were filmed and the activity level was defined for this study as the mean distance covered per 10-second exposure. This kind of measure was comparable to the measures used in studies of open field behavior of animals and repeated, albeit more sophisticatedly, in several earlier studies (Barker, 1930; Dow, 1933; Swinton, 1934; Ellis and Pryor, 1959; and Hutt, Hutt, and Ounsted, 1963).

As a pilot study, Wuellner was interested in checking whether the system could differentiate the activity of two age groups because previous research showed decrease in activity with age (Lehman and Witty, 1927; Van Alstyne, 1932). Also by separating the data for boys and girls he could check the general finding that males are more active than females.

Wuellner rearranged this play room so that although some elements were familiar they were recombined to produce a novel arrangement of the room. He then filmed nine fifteen minute sessions at ten-second intervals. Given repeated sessions together with age and sex as independent variables, a three way analysis of variance revealed five significant effects. Five year olds were significantly more active (1.16 yds. per exposure) than four year olds (.86 yards per exposure), and boys (1.10 yds/exposure) more active than girls (.88 yards per exposure). However, these sample differences were preempted in the analytical sense by the existence of interactions with the repeated sessions. Fig. 3.1 shows the age × sessions interaction and Fig. 3.2 the sex × sessions interaction. Trend analysis confirmed the fact that the trend lines were not parallel and that the statistical analysis could reveal patterns in the data.

Manipulating Activity

Fortuitously, Wuellner engaged in an experimental manipulation of the setting after six sessions. He borrowed a novel piece of apparatus from another nursery school in the university and introduced it after the sixth session. The apparatus was introduced to determine whether statistical analysis of the data produced by the fisheye system would detect differences in the children's behavior.

Subjective observation of the children showed diffuse activity through a play room filled with play objects until the novel object was introduced. Then behavior was concentrated on the novel object and locomotor activity was reduced. This was confirmed by the statistical analyses.

Trend analysis of both the initial six sessions and all nine sessions revealed that the novel play object markedly disturbed the trends. During the first six sessions the five-year-old children were uniformly more active than four-year-olds, although the activity of both dropped over time. The introduction of the novel object modified the behavior of the five-year-olds. Their activity dropped rapidly to the level of the four year olds and stayed there for the remaining sessions.

The sex × session interaction on the other hand showed a significant difference in linear and quadratic components of the trend between boys and girls before the introduction of the novel object. Boys were like girls, relatively inactive during the first session and then were markedly more active until their relative activity level once again approximated that of the girls when the novel object was introduced.

These findings were a rich by-product for a study that had as its main intent to see whether the camera and data analysis system were sensitive enough to be worth developing. Firstly, the study did not confirm the notion that older meant less active. However, it did support the finding that occurs time and again in human and animal literature that males are more active than females.

The most interesting finding resulted from the manipulation of the collative properties of the setting. Introducing the novel object concentrated the behavior on the new item. This notion was dealt with more extensively in the treatment of preferences (Chapter 3), but it was the first clear identification of the potent influence of one of the collative properties of novelty, complexity and dissonance in the data generated by the laboratory.

Even more fortuituously it occurred in a situation that affected boys and girls differently. Although older and male children were more active in general, boys were not more active than girls in the session when the arrangement of the apparatus was new (session 7) or when there was an unfamiliar object in the room. It looked as though boys lost interest in the recombined apparatus very rapidly and thereafter engaged in far more locomotor activity until an unfamiliar item was again introduced. It is as if they preferred movement in space to engagement with the familiar objects.

This propensity on the part of the males to engage in activity when their attention is not captured by a novel object or event may well be at the root of the hyperactivity problem—a male child problem. Boys are either less compliant to the task demands of a setting or exhaust the attractiveness of an object or setting sooner than do girls and are thereby forced into extraneous activity sooner.

Unfortunately Wuellner filmed only three sessions with the novel apparatus, and it is not possible to determine whether the earlier higher activity of boys would have been restored as the novel object became familiar —a phenomenon the above formulation would predict.

In an attempt to make his studies of activity more inclusive, Wuellner increased the number of derived measures and presented more data from the pilot study of the activity of children in the play room (Wuellner, Witt, and Herron, 1970). In addition to the locomotor activity scores reported in Fig. 3.1 and 3.2 he derived two additional locomotor activity scores and three scores describing the use of the play equipment located in the room. These scores were: the time on equipment, the number of visits to equipment, and the average duration of a visit (see Appendix A:II for derivations). These sets of scores were intercorrelated to determine which measures were so highly correlated that they could be ignored as redundant and which were measuring different dimensions of activity.

In general the scores were not highly interrelated arguing that all the scores were measuring different aspects of a child's movement patterns. Only one variable, "Total distance moved" seemed redundant. It had high correlations with "velocity of movement" and "number of intervals moving" which seemed to be a reflection of the arithmetic relation between these two measures. Obviously, the distance covered is a function of how fast children moved on average, and for how long they moved.

Activity Norms Needed

This first study pointed out clearly the need for norms and it was in the minds of all concerned that extensive normative work in different settings and with different children was an important next step. The capacity to characterize the normal limits of activity and to chart the development of activity would have provided a stable base of understanding concerning activity. Hypo-activity and the burgeoning hypo-kinetic diseases were actively being discussed at this time, but there were no real tools available to describe the activity of normal North American children. By the same token there was a lively interest in hyperactivity, and yet there were no real measures against which hyperactivity could be objectively compared.

Unfortunately normative developmental studies are expensive and despite several efforts to obtain funds for this purpose throughout the period this research was being carried out, none were successful. So the work on activity continued in the absence of any clear ideas as to what was a normal activity level.

The pressures of the labs funding base periodically directed the work away from fundamental questions about children in general to questions about special children—the wards of departments of mental health. These pressures were polite and subtle—emphasizing the need for information useful in the fight to deliver decent care to the mentally retarded and mentally ill. Thus there is a repeated theme throughout this chapter. A research question was asked in a general way about children and their capacities, and the procedures were then applied to some classification of exceptional children using a comparative paradigm.

Activity of Downs Syndrome Children

The first comparative study was conducted by Linford *et al.* (1971). They compared the free play activity of children exhibiting Down's Syndrome (DS) with that of normals. The study exploited the opportunity to place young normals and children with DS into a situation where their play activities could be objectified—the Play Research Laboratory in the Children's Research Center.

While the study was motivated on the one hand by merely wishing to compare and contrast the two groups, there were data extant that suggested that retardates were less able to structure their own environment than normals (Tizard, 1964).

The study was established with eleven children exhibiting DS whose chronological age ranged from four through eight years and whose mental age was an average 3-5 years. The contrast subjects were four groups of normal children (total N = 32) whose chronological ages ranged between 3.5 and 5 years. These children attended the C.R.C. nursery school and were of above average mental age (MA). However, in one sense the comparisons drawn made clinical sense in that the exceptional children were merely contrasted with their normal peers. It was not the intent to try to tie differences in behavior to exact differences in CA and MA, but to provide insights into the management of free range activity of two roughly comparable samples of children.

Five dependent variables were derived from the film for each subject for each of ten 15-minute sessions. The sampling rate was one exposure per ten seconds resulting in 90 exposures per session. The individual scores were derived as shown in Appendix A:III and the group means for the DS and the normal children plotted against session to show the trends over time. While no further statistical analysis was undertaken, the data presented by Linford *et al.* tells a convincing story.

Fig. 4.1 shows that the normals were consistently active at a level of about 1.3 yards per frame. The DS children's mean activity was more erratic, and they covered approximately only one half the distance per frame than the normals. Analysis of the other distance covered variables (Figs. 4.2, 4.3) showed that they moved less often and when they did move, they moved more slowly than normals.

When the usage of apparatus rather than free space is considered, again the DS children were markedly less active (Fig. 4.4). Finally, when the usage of individual items of apparatus was analyzed there were marked differences in popularity of the items and a rank difference correlation between normals and DS children was exactly zero.

Linford *et al.*, having described the two groups of children, and recognizing the problems in studying non-equivalent groups, went on to speculate what these findings meant. The first obvious point was that the energy expended on activity by DS children when they are left to play was far less than that expended by normals. The DS children were hypokinetic and the interrelation between their natural fitness levels and their propensity to play actively needed investigating. This finding was in line with earlier findings

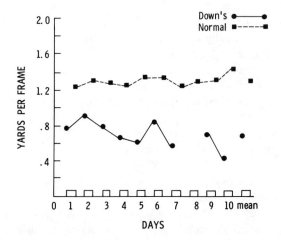

Fig. 4.1: Average distances moved by groups of normal children and those with Down's Syndrome during ten sessions at play.

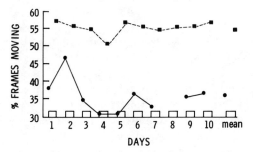

Fig. 4.2: Mean percentage of frames spent moving by groups of normal children and those with Down's Syndrome.

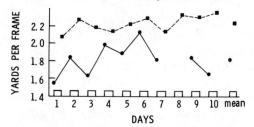

Fig. 4.3: Mean velocity of movement of two groups of children, one normal and the other exhibiting Down's Syndrome.

that retarded children were less able to structure their activity spontaneously. Linford *et al.* suggest

[that] low or non-verbal child may have, as a general behavioral pattern, the tendency to make more use of models than the normal child who is used to behavioral control by means of verbal stimuli, [this] may explain the

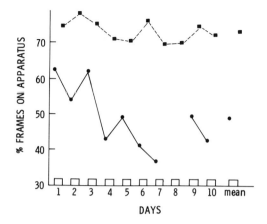

Fig. 4.4: Mean percentage of play time spent on play apparatus by normal children and those exhibiting Down's Syndrome.

greater free space usage by the Down's Syndrome child. Thus the time that they spent in free space could well have been utilized for the purpose of matching what the other children were doing in order to imitate them.

The hypothesis that the apparatus was too complicated or of no interest to the DS children so they did not engage with the apparatus is not very appealing. There was a large variety of items and some items were as popular with DS children as with the normals or more so. However, while there were items that attracted their interest, the usage patterns were obscure.

This study demonstrated that the system was sensitive enough to pick up differences in the spontaneous behavior of retardates—a welcome demonstration since the bulk of the foregoing research and research methods was aimed at criterion skills and managed behaviors and had ignored free activity. It pointed to the fact that when not provided with structured activity DS children were hypokinetic.

The hypokinetic behavior of these children stimulated Linford and Duthie (1970) to ask whether DS children could generate levels of energy expenditure that were approximately normal. They chose two DS children and used an operant schedule to reinforce performance of a set of three high energy expenditure tasks. They used a simplified system of circuit training, more customarily used by athletes for physical conditioning, to raise the palpated heart-rate of the two DS children. The children rotated round the circuit of exercises that involved running, lifting, and climbing as fast as they could for a certain period. They were rewarded with food that had been shown to be remarkably effective in other settings (mayonnaise sandwich for Geoff, and "M & Ms" or "Smarties" plus smiles for Kathy).

By judicious shaping of the behavior the DS children soon began to work hard at the circular task and both routinely elevated their heart-rate to 180 beats/minute. When there were very clear extrinsic contingencies tied to their behavior, the two DS children could generate "normal" levels of energy expenditure. It seemed that when DS children are left on their own they are inactive not because of inherent physiological limitations on activity, but because other factors, most probably of a psychological nature, do not reinforce active engagement with the setting.

The research at this point changed its themes as the investigators sought for the funds and the methods necessary for more far reaching studies of free ranging activity. Within the next few years these methods were developed (see Chapter 1) but funds were not, and the laboratory turned to research involving the study of aberrant activity levels and the periodicity of activity. These themes could be investigated with the resources available.

Hyperactivity and Hyperkinesis

Hyperactivity is an adult complaint about children (and some other adults). Children are presented by teachers as being excessively active in the confines of a classroom or dayroom. They fail to sit still and attend. They talk, turn, wriggle, and are easily distracted. They disrupt their peers. Parents complain that the child is too active at home and behaves badly in structured elements of the family life. They are a nuisance at the meal table, will not concentrate on their chores, and are restless at bedtime. Hyperactive children become management problems for adults when the required or expected activity is not produced by a child.

Given the above complaints, a label has been attached to children causing the complaints. They are classified as hyperactive. The word has become fashionable and large numbers of children are now "hyperactive". In the United States it is estimated that from 3 to 5% of elementary school age children are hyperactive (Stewart *et al.*, 1966; Anon., 1971; Howell, Rever, and Scholl, 1972). A large proportion of these children are treated medically by the prescription of amphetamine drugs that paradoxically often reduce the problem, albeit at the cost of some side effects like anorexia. Despite the success in treating hyperactivity pharmacologically, the mechanisms causing it are not well understood, and there is clear dissatisfaction with a method of treatment that only erases symptoms.

The Children's Research Center was one site where hyperactivity was actively researched in order to try to establish the etiology or etiologies of the behavior. Karlsson (1971) in her doctoral research at the Children's Research Center clearly identified the various possible etiologies and set about using the behavior of hyperactive children in informal settings to sharpen the notions concerning its causes. Karlsson proposed that hyperactivity was an awkward term which obstructed progress in the field. She also condensed the many proposed etiologies of the complained of behavior into two major groupings. These were:

> *Hyperkinetic* behavior is the excessive activity displayed as a result of some organic malfunction or infirmity, e.g. brain-damage, neurological impairment, which are often associated with mental retardation. Thus, excessive activity is one symptom in the hyperkinetic syndrome, others being the neurological signs of impairment. This corresponds to the primary hyperactivity described by Howell, Rever and Scholl (1972).
>
> *Hyperactive* behavior refers to excessive activity shown by a child who has been diagonsed as "normal" organically and intellectually. Thus hyperactivity may be an intolerably high activity level in some children created by the naturally occurring variability among children. This corresponds closely to Howell, Rever and Scholl's (1972) definition of secondary hyperactivity.

Hyperkinesis seems to result from neurological or physiological deviancies on the part of the child that arise from trauma or inherited faults. Thus neonatal difficulties may induce brain dysfunction that disturbs or retards the normal development of the mechanisms that influence activity. In fact MBD (minimal brain dysfunction) is often used as a diagnostic label when a child is hyperkinetic. Alternatively the child may have inherited chromosomal disorders that determine activity level. These kinds of disorders are not very satisfactorily dealt with except by compensatory interference with the central nervous system via drugs. Reduction of symptoms is all that can actually be done in these cases.

Another set of causes has surfaced recently. Deviations in tissue chemistry, particularly sugar metabolism (Crook, 1974; Walker, 1974) seem to induce the restless and diffuse activity that characterises the hyperkinetic child. Restoring individual tissue chemistry reduces the symptoms. For example, in one year Crook found specific food sensitivities in 55 children who were hyperkinetic. Sixteen were sensitive to cane sugar, and its removal from their diets alleviated the symptoms. In one case the hyperkinetic symptoms would appear within 5 minutes of ingesting cane sugar. These deviant reactions, provided they can be discovered, suggest easy solutions.

Hyperactivity, on the other hand, is neither explained not treated as satisfactorily as hyperkinesis. There are several hypothesized etiologies, and each suggests a somewhat different approach to treating the problem apart from masking their symptoms with drugs.

Etiology of Hyperactivity

The most obvious explanation for hyperactivity among those free of organic deficits is that it is normal. In every sphere of human behavior there is variability among people. It is to be expected that the propensity to emit activity despite constraints will vary. So it is normal for some children to be more active than others. This would imply that while inconvenient, it should be expected and planned for. The constraints on being active should be altered to accommodate a normal range of activity rather than altering the internal environment of an otherwise healthy child by means of drugs.

A related explanation postulates that hyperactive children have higher than normal needs for stimulation. Their hyperactive behavior may be generated by a continuous search for information within themselves and their immediate environment. As has been identified in this work, it has been suggested that this is modulated by the reticular system and for convenience has been labelled as an arousal-seeking phenomenon. Natural variations among children or perturbations of the arousal system may require these children to emit relatively large quantities of information-seeking behavior. When this cannot be tolerated by adults they produce the complaints that lead to the labelling of these children as hyperactive. Another explanation is that the behavior of the child labelled hyperactive is learned behavior. The child for one reason or another thrives on the increased attention generated by inappropriate behavior. Such a child's behavior is adaptive and is maintained by the social reinforcement inherent in the setting. Here of course management would require the analysis of the contingencies sustaining the behavior.

The remaining notion is more complex because it involves the interaction of several features. Schulman, Kasper, and Throne (1965) have shown that the mean optimal activity level of hyperactive children is not greater than that of normal children. However, they argue that as children move through their day they pass from one setting to another which vary in their activity task demands. Some impose restrictions on activity, and in others a greater activity level is appropriate. Normal children, it seems, can modulate, or have learned to modulate, their activity to comply with the task demand characteristics. Hyperactive children may not have learned or may be incapable of modulating their activity. They are not more active on average, but cannot tolerate deviations from their own mean optimal activity level for very long.

In a sense, this explanation characterizes hyperactivity as an incapacity to inhibit activity when necessary. It coincides well with the notions that hyperactivity is often merely "inappropriate activity" (Werry and Sprague, 1970). It is in agreement with reports that hyperactive children have low tolerance of frustration, and are impulsive with unreliable self-control, and that they "exhibit an activity level that is relatively continuous; it is not turned off in inappropriate situations" (Howell, Rever, and Scholl, 1972). This explanation suggests that the structure of the setting must be altered to allow children with differing capacities to inhibit their activity to function independently.

Unfortunately, in our society the mystification of the medical profession has profitably placed the onus for the management of the hyperactive child on the medical practitioner and the drug industry (Lennard, *et al.*, 1970, Brand, *et al.*, 1970). Very large numbers of children are currently being medicated, and there is no doubt that the children as a result are more tractable. However, the question remains, "What causes hyperactivity?" and "At what cost is this tractability bought?" Much of the work in this chapter bears on these questions.

Karlsson (1972) went on, after sorting out the extant hypothesized etiologies, to ask whether hyperactive children who behaved differently in formal settings also behaved differently in informal settings. Adults' complaints about these children are usually made concerning their behavior in formal settings and no data was available about their behavior in informal settings—since these settings are usually unsupervised by adults and therefore less likely to generate complaints. Important data concerning the etiology of hyperactivity could be generated from observing hyperactive children in playful informal settings.

Karlsson also noted that manipulating of an informal setting and observing the resulting behavior could sharpen the hypotheses concerning the causes of hyperactivity. She posed two questions: "1) Can measures of activity in the informal setting differentiate hyperactive from normal children? 2) If there are differences, can they account for hyperactivity in terms of the various etiologies?"

Manipulating Hyperactivity

The first question was answered by testing for differences in observed activity between normal and hyperactive children in the Play Research Laboratory. Answering the second required manipulating the play setting and determining whether the play behaviors of the two classes of children were modulated differently. The complexity of the social setting and the physical setting was varied. The social setting was manipulated by observing the subjects at play either alone or in the company of three playmates chosen from the same grade and same school. The physical setting was manipulated by placing in it either a rolling ball lever-operated maze game, or the maze game together with a selection of play apparatus designed to elicit gross motor activity. Each subject participated in eight sessions on a counterbalanced schedule so that each of four conditions was replicated once. The conditions were:

1) low physical complexity in a group
2) low physical complexity alone
3) high physical complexity in a group
4) high physical complexity alone.

The subjects by virtue of their diagnosis provided the crucial sampling variable; hyperactive versus normal. They were eight white males between 8 and 11 years of age and in third or fourth grade of the public school system. Four of the children were normal and four hyperactive according to the selection criteria, and the study was run with double-blind safeguards. Selection was made by interviewing principals of schools to determine which classes in his school had children in them who had been referred to him for behavioral problems involving hyperactivity. Then teachers were asked to complete a checklist for all the white males in their class. This checklist was constructed from the two checklists customarily used in the diagnosis of hyperactivity. Seventeen of the items were from Factor 1 of the Quay-Peterson (1967) Behavior Problem Checklist which is used to indicate hyperactivity. A further 8 items that comprise the Hyperactivity Factor IV in Conners checklist (1969) were included. (See Appendix F.)

The checklist was used in this fashion to identify contrasting children. The hyperactive group had to be conspicuously hyperactive in the classroom setting, and the normal children clearly not so. Also the hyperactive children could not be on medication. The sampling constraints were difficult to honor because hyperactive children were in short supply for the drug studies being undertaken in the town. However, four suitable boys were found who were clearly rated hyperactive by their teachers. Their mean checklist score (from a possible 58) was 42.5, while the contrast group selected from the same classrooms had a mean checklist score of 3.75. This difference was very clearly significant ($t = 6.85$ $p < .01$).

The classes of measures used to describe the activity in the playroom are by now familiar. The camera system was used to generate seven variables, the heart rate telemetry system was used to develop two variables and subjective observation was used to develop another. (See Appendix A:V for operational definitions) These three measuring systems were used because it is clear that hyperactivity includes not only gross activity or energy expenditure but also elements of impulsivity and distractibility. Accordingly, many measures were used to try to capture the many interrelated attributes of hyperactive behavior. "Activity" is not a unifactored phenomenon (Atkinson, 1970) and measures of locomotion, energy expenditure, velocity, and attention to and interaction with equipment, together with the variance statistics derived from those measures, are all important parameters of hyperactivity. Thus it was expected that these measures would, when analyzed collectively in a multivariate procedure, discriminate between the interactive effects of the environmental manipulations and etiology. The expected relative behavior patterns were specified beforehand. They were:

1. The Energy Hypothesis.
   If the hyperactive child's problem was an inability to inhibit a need for activity, *or* because the child fell into the "hyperactive" portion of the normal activity distribution of the population, then his activity level would be consistently higher than that of normal children under any and all social

and physical conditions. Some variation would occur in the activity levels of the normal children along with changes in conditions. These children were expected to reduce their activity level when the stimulus level was very low, in keeping with the compliance demand characteristics of the play environment. When stimulus level was higher their activity was expected to rise in order to utilize the various aspects of the environment.

2. The Arousal Level Hypothesis.

If the arousal level explanation was appropriate, variations in physical complexity would elicit different types of behavior. When the apparatus was simple and the child was alone, the stimulus input encountered in the environment would be at its lowest. The hyperactive *S*s activity level would rise relative to the normal *S*s. The increased activity would be a compensation created by the hyperactive child's differential inability to tolerate a reduced arousal level, and would result from an attempt to elicit stimuli from the environment. When the environment was of high complexity the high arousal level of the hyperactive *S*s would be accommodated and the task demands for higher activity would be honored by the normals. Little differences between activity levels of the normal and hyperactive children were expected in the more complex conditions. The *S*s encountered each condition twice, and it would be expected that the first encounter would be more arousing than the second encounter with the same condition. The activity of the hyperactive *S*s would be expected to increase markedly in the second encounter especially in the low complexity condition as a result of familiarity with the environment.

3. The Learned Behavior Hypothesis.

This explanation would predict that if peers were social reinforcers of the hyperactive behavior in the child's environment, then the hyperactivity would only be emitted when they (the peers) were present. When the hyperactive child was playing alone, there would be no difference in activity levels between him and the normal children.

4. No Differences.

A fourth hypothesis was in order to explain the case of no differences between groups according to etiology being found in any of the four environmental conditions. It would mean acceptance of the null hypothesis that no difference existed in the compliance activity of hyperactive and normal children in four manipulated play situations. This would mean that hyperactivity is situationally determined i.e. produced in "formal" settings.

Analysis of the data produced by the Karlsson study confirmed what had been found in other studies (Wuellner, 1969; Witt, 1971) that the variables were intercorrelated (mean absolute $r = .51$ and range $-.89$ to $+.95$) and that 22 of the 66 correlations were significant ($p < .05$ for 6 degrees of freedom, $r = .62$). Inspection of the matrix allowed highly redundant variables to be eliminated to simplify the cognitive gymnastics necessary when considering any multivariate factorial design. Eight variables were retained to represent the quantity and variability of the children's behavior. The quantity measures were:

> Total distance moved
> Proportion of intervals spent moving

Distance moved when moving
Heartrate.

The variability measures were:

Intravariance of movement
Total number of visits to apparatus
Observation score
Standard Deviation of Heartrate

The analysis proved difficult because the degrees of freedom for error $(2(n-1) = 6)$ were less than the number of dependent variables. Further, the number of possible effects inherent in the factorial design was large (15). The simplification process and explanations are reported in detail in Karlsson (1972). In brief, however, the group of six variables (the number permitted by the degrees of freedom for error) that best discriminated the physical and social complexity interaction was sought by repeated runs. Since there were 28 possible combinations of six variables the searching process was short-circuited by using inspection of the correlation matrix, the relations manifested in other studies (Witt, 1971, Ellis, Witt, Reynolds, and Sprague, 1974) and, the step-down analyses in preceding runs.

Finding the combination of variables that best discriminated the interaction of the physical and social complexity manipulations was considered logically important. If the experimental manipulations were not powerful enough to influence the children's behavior then it would have been difficult to interpret the presence or absence of their interaction with the etiology of the children. The first step in the analysis then was to determine which combination of variables reliably discriminated the effects of a physical and social complexity interaction.

The six variables that produced the most reliable multivariate F ($F = 124.46$, 1 & 6 df, p < .07) were: total distance moved (TOTD), proportion of intervals spent moving (PRPM), total number of visits (VSTS), distance moved when moving (DMWM), intravariance of movement (INTM), and the observation score (OBSV).

When apparatus was added four of the dependent variables increased (TOTD, PRPM, VSTS, OBSV). This indicated that the apparatus produced more activity, but that the activity was slightly slower and less variable (i.e. there were reductions in INTM and DMWM). When playmates were added all aspects of the children's behavior were intensified. Addition of apparatus to the alone condition elicited a large increase (four variables (TOTD, PRPM, VSTS, OBSU) in activity while the addition of apparatus to the group condition produced a considerable increase in visits to the apparatus (VSTS) but little other effect. Thus, when etiology was ignored, there were differences in the way the children behaved in the different environmental conditions. These differences could be reliably discriminated (the F ratio was very large — 124) taking into account the small number of subjects.

Given the logically required effect of the environmental manipulations, the crucial test of their interaction with etiology followed. There was no significant multivariate effect ($F = 9.52$ with 1 and 6 df, p < .24). Inspection of the five other analyses showed this F ratio to be the highest and in not one analysis was even the main effect for etiology significant. Although the power of a test with such a small sample size is low, the disparity in the critical F ratios (124:9) and the very consistent lack of any etiology effects (not one of the 48 F tests involving an etiology effect approached significance) argues strongly for the acceptance of the null hypothesis. To summarize and answer the first question, although the hyperactive children were markedly more active in the classroom than their normal peers, and the environmental manipulations did modulate all the children's behavior, the hyperactive children still played like normal children on a variety of objective measures.

Karlsson, taking the advice of Hummel and Sligo (1971) and Cramer and Bock (1966), and after finding no differences using multivariate statistics, proceeded to univariate analyses. To cut a long story short, Karlsson found that only one variable, the subjectively determined observation score that was designed to reflect the number of episodes in a child's play, could differentiate the behavior of the hyperactives. This variable produced a significant etiology main effect ($F = 8.17$ with 1 and 6 df, p < .03). Summing overall conditions the hyperactive children produced more episodes (21) or themes than the normals, who produced only 14.

The second question asked whether patterns of differences in the behavior of hyperactives and normals in differently structured informal settings could sharpen the hypotheses concerning etiology of hyperactivity. Of the patterns of difference specified beforehand, only one, no differences, fitted the findings. The absence of differences in the playroom and the presence of large differences in the classroom suggested that hyperactivity is situationally determined. In the playroom there was no generalized excess of activity. In the classroom the problem most likely stems from the failure to comply with external constraints. Thus, on all the measures the normal children and hyperactive children behaved alike in the absence of constraint. In constrained situations the hyperactive children do not or cannot inhibit their behavior and so emit the behavior of which adults complain.

As mentioned, hyperactives were shown to be different from normals on only one variable, the subjective observation score (Karlsson 1971). Under all environmental conditions the hyperactives sustained series of response organized around a single intention or theme for less time than the normals. The objective content of their behavior was similar to that of the normals, but the thematic content was different. Interestingly, the observation score was the only subjective measure in the study and thus paralleled the essentially subjective nature of a teacher rating scale. It seems that humans can differentiate the hyperactive children when asked to count the number of times they change the theme of their behavior.

To summarize, Karlsson's finding of a subjective difference in the behavior of hyperactives no matter what the setting and no objective differences between hyperactives and normals in the different informal settings, sharpen the Werry and Sprague (1970) definition of hyperactivity. They classified it as a disorder of movement which results in "conflict with the social environment due to amount of movement and/or its inappropriateness to the situation." It seems more accurate to define hyperactivity as resulting from a "child's conflict with the demands for compliance to the demands of a social setting that results in the emission of socially inappropriate responses (Karlsson, 1971)."

The observation score was designed to measure the "distractibility" of the children but in retrospect, "distractibility" only makes sense to another person requiring the child to stay on task. When there is no defined, "on-task" behavior, as in an informal setting, one has to ask, "Distracted from what?" This study then shows that the hyperactive children change themes far more often than do normals. This may result from low capacity to maintain attention to the task, or a more rapid exhaustion of the interesting content in an episode. The latter corresponds to the "arousal-level" hypothesis that these children have a higher than normal need for information flow, and in honoring that need emit the inappropriate behaviors of which teachers complain. Two rival management procedures are suggested by this. The "distractibility hypothesis" requires the elimination of extraneous interesting stimuli competing with a required task. The "high information need hypothesis" requires the delivery of more information per unit time than normal.

Methylphenidate & Activity

The next three studies were all motivated by the increased concern for the growing number of children who were being drugged for the behavior problems of distractibility, fidgeting, and social disruptiveness that are often collectively called hyperactivity.

It has been noted that stimulant drugs exert a paradoxical effect on hyperactive children. When drugged they are quieter, less active and their on-task performance improves. One of the drugs marketed, methylphenidate (Ritalin[R]), is described by the manufacturer, "as a mild stimulant, an antidepressant which brightens the mood and improves performance (CIBA 1967)." This drug has become popular and several researchers have found beneficial effects, however, there is some evidence that it deleteriously influences learning and memory (Sprague and Sleator, 1973).

While the drug improved the capacity of the child to comply with the constraints of the classroom, very little was known concerning its effects in informal settings. Should the drug reduce the activity of the child outside the classroom then there is the clear possibility that the cognitive and social development of the child that comes through play will be retarded. Since there was no data on the effect of methylphenidate on informal behaviors three experiments concerning the effect of the drug on the play behavior of hyperactives were conducted. They all asked whether the ingestion of methylphenidate produced discriminable differences in the behavior of hyperactives in the informal setting.

In the pilot study eight children (Mean age 9.4 years) from special classes showing antisocial, distractible, and hyperactive behavior were used. The subjects had participated in other drug studies previously but had not been medicated for several months. The children were familiarized for two sessions in the play room and then played for four fifteen-minute experimental sessions. The children played in randomly selected groups of four in the play research laboratory stocked with a variety of play and climbing apparatus. During each session the camera was run and three dependent variables— total distance moved, number of intervals moving, and intravariance of movement were derived (see Appendix A:VI).

Three hours prior to each session the children swallowed either a capsule containing .30 mg methylphenidate/kg body weight, or placebo. These two treatments were replicated in counter-balanced order and the data analyzed in a subjects × drug level multivariate design. The multivariate effect for drug versus placebo was not significant ($F = 2.98$, p $<$ .16 with 3 and 4 df). Thus the three variables combined in their most discriminating combination could not separate the effects of ingesting .30 mg/kg methylphenidate on free-ranging activity.

While the methylphenidate had been shown to influence the behavior in settings characterized by a task or required behavior it did not seem to produce an effect in a play setting. These effects can be reconciled by assuming that methylphenidate acts to increase the child's responsiveness to the task demand characteristics in the setting. This responsiveness was labelled the "tractability" of the child by Korb (1972).

The "tractability" explanation argues that the child when under the influence of methylphenidate intensifies task related behavior. This intensified behavior is noticeable in structured settings and is classified as improvement. In an informal setting the demand characteristics are diffuse, and the child by not being driven in a particular direction does not change behavior whether medicated or not. What parents and teachers may note as a decrease in a child's activity level after ingesting methylphenidate may really just be an improvement in other areas such as mood and attentiveness, or tractability.

The pilot study showed that noxious side effects on the informal behavior of hyperactives were not detected at a dosage of .30 mg/kg body weight. Because of this a larger second study was planned to probe for a dosage effect, to study the children's on-task performance and to capture a wider group of play behaviors. Since medical practitioners systematically vary the dosage to generate the desired effect, it seemed necessary to generate wide a range of dosages that spanned the common range of doses. Secondly, the possible contextual modification of hyperactivity required the analysis of the behavior of the children in formal situations with a specific task demand. This second experiment was run parallel to a laboratory learning study during the time the children played in the playroom while "waiting" for the taxi to take them back to school. Finally, the multi-factored nature of activity (Atkinson, 1970) suggested that as large a variety of dependent variables as possible should be used.

Despite attending to all these methodological concerns a procedural error was made that vitiated the experiment. However, it has something to teach us. The twelve hyperactive children were assigned randomly to groups of four and were run through the replicated conditions of no drug, placebo, .15, .30 and .45 mg/kg together. While the order of presentation was counter-balanced the composition of the groups was not.

The early results were complex and a significant Group × Trial × Dosage interaction was found ($F = 1.34$, p < .05 with 72 and 233 degrees of freedom) for a multivariate treatment of the nine dependent variables measured (see Appendix A:IV).

In this experiment it is not sufficient to find just one cell discriminably different from one other. Since there were five drug levels, for the results to be meaningful there should have been clear patterns in the cell means that represented the trends created by the additive effect of the placebo and the increasing dosage effects.

Alternatively some "all or none" effect may appear at a dosage level, in which cases there is no difference among those below threshold, and among those above. However, no such pattern appeared in a post-hoc ordering of the centroids created by using weighted combinations of each individual's scores. The weightings were produced by using the two significant discriminant analyses that allowed the separation of at least two of the cells in the group × trials × dosage interaction. The centroids, which are similar to multivariate means, were in complete disarray. Neither the "additive" effect nor an "all or none" effect was apparent; the ordering of the cells seemed random.

Finally, Witt (1971) decided to test the hypothesis that the interaction was produced by another effect that had been scrambled by separating the scores due to dosage. He had observed that the children tended to continue the games and activities that they had been playing the day before when the 10 minute play session was up (the taxi arrived). Thus the thread running through the data was what he called the "group life" effect. Since the same children got to know each other and they always played together, the activity of each group followed its own separate trend according to the evolution of themes that carried over from one session to the next. He tested the notion that the effect was caused by the order of presentation.

To simplify the analysis, Witt did not consider every variable, but tested only the variable with the highest standardized discriminant weight — total distance moved — in a group × sessions analysis. The result was highly significant (univariate $F = 8.98$, p < .01 with 18 and 81 df). Each group had its own pattern of activity. In fact inspection of the distances moved showed that groups 1 and 3 had almost symmetrically opposite patterns of activity, yet they were both assigned to the same order of dosage administration. Order had been brought to chaos. The effects seem best described by a group-life effect and not by any influence due to drugs. In fact dosage seemed to be a very minor influence compared to the effect of peers — another indicator that peers are a most powerful source of variance in the play setting.

At this point the original question had not yet been satisfactorily answered. The pilot study suggested that .30 mg/kg of methylphenidate had no effect. The second study had only shown that group-life was a far more powerful effect than methylphenidate. A third study was therefore undertaken (Ellis *et al.*, 1974). This study broadened the range of dosages to .10, .30 and 1.00 mg/kg and nine children aged 8-10 were used. These children had been referred to the CRC's research physician who after careful screening decided it was in the hyperactive child's best interest to undergo trial medication with methylphenidate. These children were being maintained in the normal school system and underwent a double-blind set of four month-long trials of daily dosing with the amounts above plus a placebo.

The drug conditions were counterbalanced to form a Latin-square and children randomly assigned to each combination. Subjects were asked to play in the playroom on their own while their parents were interviewed elsewhere. The same apparatus was used in the playroom, and the camera system was used to generate the same variables as for the second study (see Appendix A: IV).

In this study dosage was the only experimental effect under test and a nine-variable single-factored multivariate analysis of variance revealed no effect (Multivariate $F = .85$, p < .67 with 27 and 39 df). Thus nine dependent variables describing a large variety of different aspects of a child's activity, even when combined to maximize their discriminatory power, could not separate the play of the children under different dosages. Furthermore none of the univariate Fs were significant. This outcome contrasts directly with reports that methylphenidate clearly affects behavior in formal settings (Sprague and Sleator, 1973).

Hyperactivity : Contextual Problem ?

Each of the four studies required the logically awkward acceptance of the null hypothesis, but the collective power of all the tests described argues strongly for that same conclusion. Taken together they show that the behavior of the hyperactive child is a problem only in the formal classroom setting.

This finding was also supported by a study of the sensitivity of parent and teacher reports (Sprague, Barnes and Werry, 1970). Teacher reports on the behavior of hyperactives were reliably sensitive to dosages of methylphenidate. However, the parent reports of the behavior during the weekends of the same study were not sensitive to the conditions of no drug, placebo, or a dosage.

Teachers in the more formal setting of the classroom could discriminate the effects of methylphenidate, whereas parents in the less formal setting of a weekend at home could not report any differences. We had conducted another series of studies that found that the effects of methylphenidate are contextually modified.

Thus hyperactivity remains only as a problem for formal settings where children are constrained to be on task. The research conducted in the Play Research Laboratory constantly reported that when at play hyperactive children were not discriminable from normal children on a large variety of measures of their behavior. The research went further in that it pointed out that there was no need to fear that the drug would inhibit active engagement with the environment when outside the classroom—the arena in which the behavior was a problem. Thus the effect of hyperactivity and the drug methylphenidate do not seem to affect energy expenditures or the activity of children. Instead hyperactivity and the effects of methylphenidate seem to involve attentional deficits. Future advances in understanding and management of hyperactivity will therefore depend on the modification of environmental factors that will allow a match between the needs of the child and those of the school system.

Periodicities in Activity

Periodicities in the activity of animals and plants have long been recognized. Seasonal variations in temperature, hours of light, available water, etc. have caused many animals to divide their time between activity and quiescence. The study of seasonal, monthly, and daily variations in activity of living things has been labelled biorhythm research.

Biorhythm research has largely concentrated upon long periodicities or cycles that are driven by external influences, usually originating in the regular events of the solar system. These events are seen to lie outside the organism, and the periodicities they produce are labelled exogenous rhythms. However, there has developed recently a concern for cycles that seem to follow repeating internal events, and this class of rhythms are endogenous.

The research reported here is part of a thrust towards the identification and explanation of cycles in man which last less than 24 hours and which are apparently endogenous in nature. The present research borrows analytical procedures developed to study cycles and has as its goal a contribution to the understanding of the activity of children freed to manifest any endogenously determined rhythms.

The research began with the observation that children seem to be active in fits and starts. Since the laboratory was concerned with hyperactivity at the time (1968–71) it seemed that this was a potential explanation for the burgeoning problem of hyperactivity. What if a child's activity was periodic and driven from within? Those children who are out of phase with their environment and unable to suppress or synchronize their periodic bursts of activity might be labelled hyperactive because their activity, by not being externally driven, would appear maladaptive.

This early question was very quickly elaborated into a theoretical model that would explain the alternation between periods of activity and quiescence.

Two sets of factors appear to act in countervailing fashion on the level of free-ranging activities in man. It is well documented that there is a homeostatic system in man that regulates the internal environment and which eliminates the disturbances created by the products of muscular activity. This system can run into debt due to local energy supplies that can be restored later. Also, there seems to be a clearly demonstrated need for man to process information, perhaps mediated by the necessity to maintain appropriate arousal (Fiske and Maddi, 1961). This may be regarded as a process of sensoristasis (Schultz, 1965) which in some circumstances may oppose the tendencies of the homeostatic mechanisms.

In an environment with complex stimuli, the drive to process information should elicit interactions that cost energy. As energy is expended and local systems run into debt, the homeostatic mechanisms will be disturbed creating a tendency for the organism to reduce the level of energy expenditure to pay-off or reduce the incurred debt. Taking into account the lag in the homeostatic mechanisms, these two factors should interact to produce rhythmic work/rest patterns. This particular interaction should occur most clearly in free-ranging situations which elicit relatively large energy expenditures, and where the interaction between the systems is not interfered with by external contingencies. This rhythmic interaction should occur in children at play in a stimulating environment calling for large muscle activity (Ellis, Wade and Bohrer, 1970).

This notion was first put to test by Wade and Ellis in 1969. Two normal

6-year old boys were asked to play in the play laboratory. The playroom was filled with apparatus designed to elicit gross motor activity, and they played either alone or paired with the other. The children were supervised by a nonreactive adult who sat and read in one corner. While playing the children wore heart rate telemeters to provide a continuous record of their heart rates throughout each session. Furthermore, a running commentary on their activity was dictated on to tape. Technical problems limited the number and completeness of the telemetered records—the robustness of the children's play generated noise on the records that occasionally masked the large deflections of the pens that were responding to the broadcast pulses triggered by the "QRS" elements of the EKG complex. However, these bursts of noise rarely obscured more than a few seconds of the record and highly reliable interpolation was possible by reference to heart beat frequencies before and after the obscured portion. Four sessions each lasting more than 60 minutes produced complete records.

These records were hand scored and the heart rates for a time series of 10 second intervals became the basic data from which activity level was to be inferred. Given that the children were relatively active and under familiar conditions, the heart rate was assumed to be an indirect measure of the energy cost of recent activity (Bradfield, Huntzicker, and Fruehan, 1969).

The mean session heart rate for both boys over all sessions was remarkably consistent ranging only from 124 to 135 beats per minute (see Table 4.1), and indicated a moderate activity level was typical for the sessions.

Table 4.1

HEART RATE OF TWO 6-YEAR OLD BOYS DURING PLAY

Subject	Duration of Session	Mean Heart Rate
1P*	60 min.	132
1P	66 min.	124
2A*	60 min.	132
2P	60 min.	135

*P = paired with others subject. A = alone.

Analysis of Periodicity : Autocorrelation

So far so good, but the task of reducing a series of at least 360 data points to periodicities now became the problem. The first analysis was conducted by Wade and Ellis on their own. They subjected the data to autocorrelation procedures and searched for periodicities by inspection of each child's autocorrellograms. The results were extremely encouraging; there seemed to be very marked periodicities of approximately 20–25 minutes in length.

At this point it is worth a digression to explain the analysis of periodicities briefly. The simplest procedure to use is an autocorrelation procedure. As the name suggests an autocorrelation results from correlating a time series with itself. First the scores are duplicated to produce two sets of identical scores. Naturally these scores correlated perfectly. One set of scores is then slipped along so that it lags behind the first set by a standard time interval, and then the scores are correlated again. The process is repeated by lagging one set of scores regularly until the reduction in degrees of freedom caused by the loss of paired scores on the ends of each set of data reduces the reliability of the correlation coefficients to unacceptable levels. When the correlation coefficients resulting from this process are plotted against the time lags it produces an autocorrellogram.

An autocorrellogram is illustrated in Fig. 4.5, and inspection of the sign and magnitude of the correlations reveals periodicities. Thus at zero lag the correlation is perfectly positive, and as serial relations between scores break down the curve tends to zero. However, if there is a periodic influence in the data the coefficients will trend on below zero as lag increases to demonstrate that the scores tend to be systematically unlike their predecessors at some given lag in the time series. This curve then reflects and passes back through zero on the way to a set of positive correlations. This now indicates that further along the time series the data are again systematically like their predecessors. Systematic swings of the correllogram reveal whether as one set of data is slid along the other the scores move regularly into and out of phase with each other. The correllogram suggests by the time lag corresponding to the peaks and troughs the length of the period influencing the data.

In Fig. 4.5 the autocorrelations were produced by lagging the scores 10 seconds at a time, the duration of each period for which the HR was counted, and continued until the lag was 50 minutes long. As can be seen the correllogram at zero lag is +1.0 and passes through zero, bottoms, and then produces a peak at about 25 minutes. The process appears to repeat itself, but

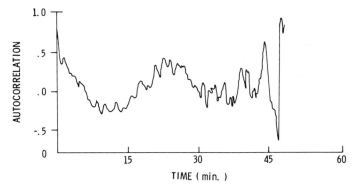

Fig. 4.5: Typical autocorrelogram of six-year old boy's heart rate during free play.

the coefficients become progressively less reliable until the random swings at 45 minutes on begin to mask the trend. This autocorrellogram suggests a strong biorhythm in the heart rate that comes full cycle in 25 minutes. In addition there is a suggestion of another shorter rhythm of about a 5–10 minute cycle superimposed upon the longer one.

Analysis of Periodicity : Spectral Analysis

Although autocorrelation is simple it relies in the final stage on inspection. It is useful in making an initial cursory treatment of the data for those who wish to reassure themselves that it is worth the effort to pursue the analysis further. The most precise method of revealing periodicities in a time series is spectral analysis. This is a statistical process that relies on theory that any complex wave form can be decomposed into a set of superimposed sine waves. Furthermore, it assumes that the processes inducing each of the periodicities are constant throughout the series. This is the assumption of stationarity.

Spectral analysis is in a sense a special type of regression analysis. A whole family of sine waves of regularly differing periods are fitted to the data and the amount of variance common to both the sine-wave and the time-series computed. The periods of a family of sine-waves is limited at one end by the length of the time series and at the other by the duration of each sample. At the long end the limit is one cycle during the time series and at the other it is one cycle per two samples.

The resulting set of estimated common variances is smoothed and plotted against the period of each of the fitted sine waves. The resulting function of a spectral analysis, a spectral density function, is shown in Fig. 4.6. Here the sine-waves ranged from 1 cycle per 60 mins. to 1 cycle per .16 mins (10 secs.). Clearly at some cycles there was more variance explained than at others. The completion of the primary analysis, however, showed regularities in the time series.

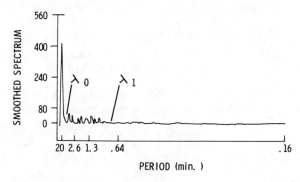

Fig. 4.6: Spectral density function of the same heart rate time series that was autocorrelated to produce Figure 4.5.

Manipulating Periodic Activity

The next question is analogous to the question that spawns a post-hoc analysis after the finding of a significant F in a more than 2-level analysis of variance. This question concerns which peaks in the spectral density function are significantly different from the base-line of random associations between data points. This baseline of random associations is called "white noise" (all frequencies have an equal chance of being represented at the same intensity) which produces a horizontal base-line through which peaks representing systematic or non-random peaks must push-through. The post-hoc tests were derived from the Grenander-Rosenblatt tests (1954) that were generated by Bohrer (1970) specifically for this application.

Bohrer's test identifies frequencies in the spectral density function that are not random fluctuation. It does so by making simplifying assumptions that can be illustrated by Fig. 4.6. From T_1 out the spectral density function was ignored and the function was tested to determine whether the section out to T_0 was white noise. This hypothesis was rejected. The test was repeated for the band width $T_0 - T_1$ and this was found to be noise. Thus the slower frequencies to the left of T_0 are significant. Thus the peaks corresponding to approximately 20 minutes in each child were found to be significant, verifying statistically, the findings generated by inspection of the autocorrellogram.

On the basis of this early work, it seemed possible that the activity level of children varied rhythmically. The data presented here show some limited evidence for the existence of rhythms of very short periods. Only two other reports of cyclic events in human behavior of this order of duration have been found in the literature. Wada (1922) noted a 45-minute activity cycle in neonates, and Frazier (1970) reports a complex of short periodicities superimposed on circadian variations in adult performance of a complex vigilance task.

Apart from intrinsic interest in this as a behavioral phenomenon predicted by taking into account two, till now, unconnected behavioral concepts, homeostasis and sensoristasis, there seems to lie ahead fruitful possibilities for investigation and application of this type of knowledge. Further research was suggested, first to replicate the findings, and then by experimental manipulation to test the assertion that the periodicity results from the interaction of the processes of homeostasis and sensoristasis. The ultimate goal of the research was a technology for manipulating the phase, period, and amplitude of the activity rhythms. The most direct application seemed to have the potential for restructuring of the children's work schedules to fit their own periodicities, particularly in those cases where the general activity level is so high that they are functionally unteachable in current school-institutional work patterns.

Growing directly from this first pilot experiment was a more complex attempt to demonstrate and modify the biorhythms presumed to manifest themselves in children's activity. If the biorhythms result from the interaction of the tendency to engage with external environment and an internal tendency towards quiescence, then manipulating the external environment should alter the periodicities. A demonstration that the rhythms were modifiable would further strengthen the argument that manipulation of the external environment had potential for management of activity in some children.

It was predicted that increasing the complexity of the play environment would increase the period length of any biorhythm (Wade, Ellis, and Bohrer, 1973), and also increase the mean activity level of the subjects (Wade and Ellis, 1971). To test this a far larger study was conducted. In this study eight boys and eight girls played in the playroom for approximately one hour. While playing the children all wore a heart-beat telemeter which allowed the continuous recording of their heart beats and thus in turn allowed inferences about their activity levels. So far, this second study had only added a far larger group of children. However, the procedures for managing the play sessions themselves were different. Firstly, children played in a room in which the complexity of the apparatus was modified so that one arrangement contained a large amount and the other far less equipment (for convenience these conditions were labelled HIQUIP and LOQUIP). It was assumed that HIQUIP was more complex, and therefore more interesting then LOQUIP. To exaggerate the complexity effect further, the children played in three group sizes (alone, in a dyad, and in a tetrad).

Table 4.2

ORDER OF PLAY SESSIONS WITH GROUP SIZES
AND APPARATUS MANIPULATIONS

Session	I	II	III	IV	V	VI	VII	Equipment Condition
Subject	1*	2	3:4	5:6:7:8	1:2	3	4	LOQUIP
Session	VIII	IX	X	XI	XII	XIII	XIV	
Subject	5	6	7:8	1:2:3:4	5:6	7	8	HIQUIP

*Numbers are subject numbers. Colon indicates subjects playing together.

The arrangement of the conditions shown in Table 4.2 produced half the data, and was replicated for the eight girls. It can be seen that when the children played in groups of four they played in the other equipment condition. This was to allow the effect of the equipment condition to be separated from the effects of the children themselves and allowed for an analysis of variance model built *a priori* to be satisfied with a minimum of 28 sessions. Note that each child played in each group size and that explicit details of the model are contained in Wade, Ellis, and Bohrer, (1973) and Wade (1971).

The procedures produced 48 records, each of which was scored to produce 120 thirty second heart beat counts.

In addition to the heart-beat scores produced by the telemetry system, a series of 30 second observation scores, time locked to the telemetry record, were also produced. An observer, hidden from the subjects, assigned ratings to the activity level observed during the preceding 30 seconds. The ratings were merely subjective global estimates of intensity and were undertaken to see whether such a simple and inexpensive system could produce reliable "intensity" information. Scores were assigned retrospectively according to the following schedule:

1. Sitting quietly, with little or no overt activity
2. Sitting and talking with small manipulative movements
3. Moving round the room at essentially a walking pace, or balancing activities
4. Running in the room or to and from the apparatus, lifting and pushing

The first question to be answered by analyses was whether the two intensities of activity measures, one subjective but direct (observation scores), and the other objective and indirect (HR telemetry scores), were measuring the same thing. Taking the telemetry scores as the criterion, the mean correlations for each condition were low (.33, .42, and .21 for alone, dyad and tetrad respectively). The coefficients were all highly reliable since the degrees of freedom were so high (range 267–417), but they were of little predictive value.

The next question asked whether increasing complexity, either by the addition of apparatus or of playmates elevated the activity level of the children. Although the observation scores tended to support the hypothesis, i.e. the higher the complexity the greater the mean observation score, there was little to be learned from them. The difficulty in forming an estimate of global intensity for 30 seconds for each of the children and their low correlation with the already validated HR scores led to their all being discarded as valueless.

The increased complexity-increased activity hypothesis was tested using the HR scores, and an analysis of variance produced only one significant effect—group size ($F = 14.5$, df 2/27, $p < 01$). A *post-hoc* analysis showed that the mean heart rate of the children playing as a tetrad was higher than that of the children playing alone.

More children in the setting produced more activity presumably because the children responded·to the continually available opportunities for interaction generated by the other children's activity. This finding is in line with the social facilitation theory propounded by Zajonc (1965) and later elaborated by other workers in the laboratory at this time (Martens, 1969, 1971; Martens and Landers, 1969a, 1969b, 1972).

The absence of an apparatus effect on intensity of activity is interesting and points to the relative potency of a peer, compared to the best efforts of a play area designer to make the environment interesting. It seemed that once the apparatus is explored, the remaining interest is generated by inter-actions with peers in the environment. This was an early demonstration of a clear preference for peers over objects that led to another study (Scholtz, 1973) that was referred to in detail in Chapter 3.

Wade, in his thesis (1971), also reported that the actual content of the activity was dependent on sex. The expected socializing of the different sex groups to play different social games reduced the sensitivity of the apparatus effect because the play objects were used differently by the boys and girls. Boys played "war games" and girls played "house." However, both sexes played "tag" games. This argues strongly for the continuance of building in a "sex effect" in the analyses in human studies. Sex role stereotyping is powerful and showed up even in these studies where each child was freed from external social stimuli and placed in a setting that presumably exerted no sex biased expectations.

The heart rate records themselves were then analyzed by spectral analysis as already described. The spectral analyses (see Fig. 4.7 & 4.8) were then tested (Bohrer, 1970) to determine whether there were significant frequency bands accounting for variance in the data. The cutoff that distinguished

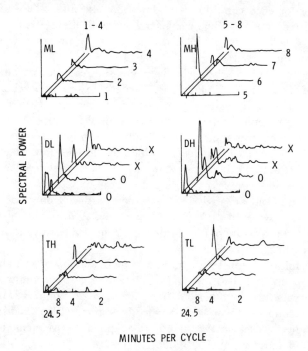

MINUTES PER CYCLE

Fig. 4.7: Spectral densities of boys' heart rates under different play condi-tions.

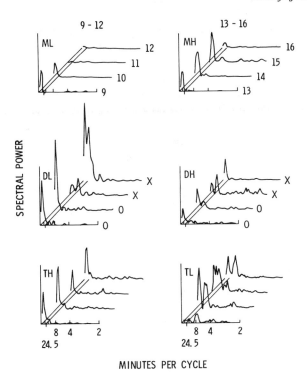

Fig. 4.8: Spectral densities of girls' heart rates under different play conditions.

meaningful periodicities from noise was 2.5 minutes per cycle. Inspection
revealed that 24.5 minutes per cycle best separated the remaining spectrum
into the fast and slow frequency bands noted in the previous study. There
was a slow frequency band in all but three subjects, but only some subjects
under some conditions exhibited a fast frequency band, suggesting that the
frequencies were independent.

The two bands seemed to be influenced by the conditions in that some
bands seemed systematically more powerful in some conditions (see Figs.
4.7 and 4.8). Inspection shows that subjects playing alone, for example, were
less periodic in their behavior, as were some individuals in the tetrad condition, and it seemed clear that dyads were most strongly periodic.

The analysis was now taken a step further to test whether the variation
among the individual density spectra was reliably influenced either independently or interactively by the size of group, playroom complexity, and sex.
This was done by building an *a priori* analysis of variance model. Subjects
were considered as a fixed effect. While this increased the sensitivity of the
design it also meant that the experimenters at this stage were willing to
accept that the outcomes could not be generalized to a population.

Fig. 4.9 shows the complexity × sex × group size interaction where each point represents four estimates of variance accounted for by the fast and slow bandwidths. In both bandwidths the typical behavior was relatively non-periodic, but in the dyad condition there was relatively far greater periodicity. Analysis of the variance in spectral power (variance accounted for by a frequency band) for the slow frequency showed that this apparent group size effect was significant. Dyads were more periodic in their behaviors than those playing alone. Thus it seemed that the children collectively exhibited a slow (about 40 minute) cycle most strongly when playing with one other child.

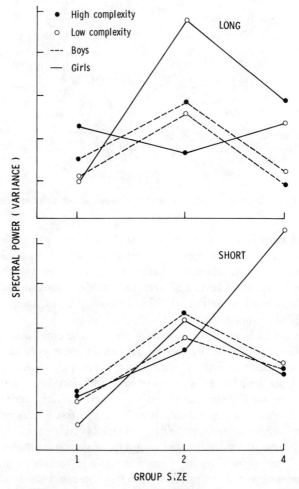

Fig. 4.9: Effect of the complexity of the play setting on the long and short cycles in the heart rates of boys and girls.

The faster frequency band also showed an effect for the number of playmates. Playing alone produced least short cycle periodicity, while the dyad condition again produced the strongest short cycle (about 15 minutes). As can be seen from Figure 4:9, one group of girls behaved differently from the other three groups, and their behavior on changing from complex to simple conditions and playing as a tetrad became markedly periodic. Why this group behaved in this way is not clear, but the increased fast cycle behavior produced a significant sex × complexity interaction.

The results of this are interesting because they confirmed the notion of periodicity and pointed to the powerful effects that the playgroup has on the activity of children. The apparatus manipulation did not produce the increase in periodicity that was predicted. There were two explanations. First, it was noted after the experiment that the different conditions had different task demand characteristics. LOQUIP naturally left more space for activity like running and chasing than did HIQUIP. Thus in LOQUIP, once the apparatus was explored, it seemed to elicit high levels of activity, whereas the additional apparatus in HIQUIP, under the same circumstances, impeded locomotor activity. Thus the procedures interacted to attenuate the predicted effects; this was certainly an experimental error.

Secondly, the model may be wrong. However, this is less plausible since the addition of complexity in the form of a playmate produced a strong effect. If the addition of apparatus and playmates increases incitement to action, then the first explanation for the lack of effect of the apparatus configuration seemed reasonable and the confounding of the available space with complex apparatus could have been avoided.

Finally, at the time this study was completed there remained the question whether the increased activity in the conditions with playmates can be explained not by the added complexity brought by others into the setting but the facilitative effect of their presence. The data presented by Scholtz in Chapter 3 was collected after this study and supported the notion that it was the added behavioral opportunities brought by playmates, rather than the facilitative effect of their mere presence, that increased activity. The more definitive experiment by Scholtz weakens the social facilitation theory of Zajonc (1965) and Martens (1975).

The original model predicted only one biorhythm resulting from the countervailing influences of incitement to action and the activity dampening effects of fatigue. The existence of two significant rhythms was unexpected. Both the pilot study and the main study found a fast and slow rhythm. It was hypothesized at the time, that these two rhythms were the result of the two processes each driving its own rhythm. The long cycle might well be the influence of the psychological processes of attention to and interaction with the environment and habituation to it. In a 60 minute period the subjects would have time to be initially excited and active, complete their interactions and fall into a period of boredom and be forced back into generating some activity to alleviate it. These three phases, activity, quiescence, activity, are neatly accommodated by the notion of three half cycles of a 40–45 minute cycle occupying a 60 minute play session.

The short cycle might best be explained by the limitations of physiological mechanisms on the production of energy for activity. The play behavior produced moderate mean energy levels, but these moderate levels resulted from the averaging of data that was oscillating about the mean. It is reasonable to argue that the 15 minute cycle resulted from alternating periods of relatively high activity and relative rest. A 7.5 minute period of relatively high activity followed by a similar period of relatively lower activity seems to be the kind of timing that would result from physiological mechanisms subjected to only minor stress.

The experiment set out to test for the existence of one biorhythm in play activity created by the interaction of two processes. It produced evidence that perhaps the two processes were not interactive, but independently drove their own rhythms—one an interest and attention/habituation and boredom cycle, and the other a relative activity/rest cycle. The experiment also revealed that these rhythms could be modulated by manipulating the external environment and thus the manifestation of the rhythms are to some extent amenable to environmental management.

Activity of Profoundly Retarded Children

The next study (Wade, 1973) followed the pattern of moving from a controlled laboratory based study on normal children to a study of exceptional children in order to determine the clinical significance of the earlier finding. Schulman *et al.* (1965) had already reported that the gross energy expenditure of hyperactives was not different from that of normals, yet hyperactivity remained an important problem. Werry and Sprague (1970) had argued that the problem was not one of activity level but the emission of inappropriate behaviors that was so disruptive. Applying this to the biorhythm work, a pertinent question follows. Perhaps hyperactivity results not from too much activity, but rather from periodicities in the activity level of the hyperactive child which are out of phase with environmental demands, and which the child is incapable of modifying.

Laufer and Denhoff (1957) point out that hyperactive children are characterized by short attention spans and a high level of distractibility. These two notions combine to suggest that hyperactives should exhibit high frequency biorhythms that are not susceptible to environmental modulation. On the other hand, it may be that the hyperactive has a normal mean activity level but is unable to suppress activity when inappropriate. In this case there would be relatively constant or unmodulated behavior and an acceptable mean energy expenditure. Normals on the other hand would be capable of inhibiting their activity in compliance with social constraints on action, and would show periodic compensatory bursts of activity.

To sharpen the hypotheses about the nature of hyperactivity, a similar biorhythm study to that reported above was conducted on hyperactive children in a clinical setting. This study addressed the problem of measuring the level and the possible periodic components in the activity of free-ranging hyperactives. It was decided to ask whether the biorhythms of hyperactives, if they existed, were susceptible to modulation by the social effects that so powerfully influenced normals.

Suitable subjects that were not on medication and who were available for study were finally tracked down in the Tinley Park Mental Health Center near Chicago. The playroom equipment, the HR monitoring system, and the staff were relocated for a week. They ran two male and three female institutionalized, profoundly retarded children. All the children were ambulatory but were classified as possessing some neurological impairment. They had a mean age of 116 months and mean IQ of 22 (ranges 91–130 and 10–28 respectively). They were selected by ratings of ward personnel, and all had a previous record of medication for hyperactivity.

The planning and execution of this study took place one year before Karlsson (1972) drew a clear distinction between primary hyperactivity or hyperkinesis and hyperactivity. The subjects were chosen to produce a clean payoff in clinical rather than theoretical terms. The subjects were institutionalized children and can retrospectively be classified as hyperkinetic not hyperactive.

The children played as dyads or tetrads (males) or as dyads and triads (females) in a room that was specially constructed to be very similar to the Play Research Lab in size and was equipped with equipment to a level of complexity somewhere between HIQUIP and LOQUIP. The analyses were similar in principle to the procedures described above, but the heart rates were computed from 20-second rather than 30-second intervals.

The mean heart rate was remarkably consistent across sex and across the various group sizes. The greatest range of mean session heart rates was only from 70–117 beats per minute. The only significant effect was that for subjects, which had been specified as a fixed effect. Thus neither sex, nor group size influenced the children's mean activity level.

The individual power spectra are shown in Fig. 4.10 and are startlingly different from those of normal children playing in very similar circumstances. The spectral density functions are remarkably flat and Bohrer's (1970) white noise test indicated that on all spectra the band for cycle duration less than 15 minutes was white noise. Some isolated spectra showed significant bandwidths for cycles shorter than 15 minutes per cycle, but the Fig. 4.10 shows that there is no interpretable pattern to these. It was concluded that there were no meaningful periodicities in the activity of this group of children.

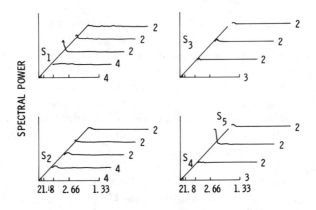

MINUTES PER CYCLE

Fig. 4.10: Spectral densities of the heart rates of individual profoundly retarded subjects at play.

Wade (1973) argued that the subjects, selected for high levels of distractibility, excitability and motor activity, behaved in an essentially random fashion uninfluenced by the behavior of other children. They moved continuously at a low to moderate level in a way that had no pattern, at least on the intensity dimension. This continuous random behavior is exactly what is detected by a noise test, in that all frequencies have an equal share of the variance. In this aspect of their behavior these children were startlingly different from normal children.

These hyperkinetic children exhibited activity that is best described as continuous, low-level random activity that was not modulated by the presence of other children. In fact the children were asocial, and it is probably this non-responsiveness and the unpredictable continuing diffuse behavior that presented such serious problems to the child care staff. This flatness of an activity spectrum might well be a specific diagnostic tool for the detection of hyperactivity resulting from neurological impairment. There was no doubt that the subjects selected were exceptional children.

After Karlsson had pointed out that the choice of subjects had prevented testing the original hypotheses about hyperactives, further attempts were made to gain funds from National Institute of Child Health and Human Development to study biorhythms in activity and establish daily norms for activity level against which hyperactive behavior could be held. This kind of work is expensive since it involves the naturalistic penetration of the lives of normal and hyperactive non-institutionalized children. The Children's Research Center and the Play Research Lab (Sprague and Ellis, 1970) were unsuccessful in obtaining these funds, and the intriguing studies that spring from all this work remain undone.

Summary

In one sense the work presented here is a mélange and the findings lack the glue of an adequate normative study of the total daily activity patterns of normal children. However, given the limits on resources, there are several findings worth summarizing.

Wuellner (1969) confirmed that young boys were more active than girls, but raised a question concerning the limits of the usual assumption that activity decreased with age. He found that five year-olds were more active than younger children. He also found evidence that the activity of boys and girls was differentially influenced by adding a novel object to the setting. The activity of the group was altered in a way that suggested that boys processed the information inherent in a setting more rapidly than girls. Boys behaved like girls when there was something new or interesting present, but broke away into high energy activity sooner than the girls after pausing to explore.

Karlsson (1972), when studying hyperactivity, raised the notion that there were many possible mechanisms driving hyperactive children. One of those was that hyperactive children had a greater need for information, or reduced extant information more quickly, and were impelled to seek information sooner than normally active children. The early Wuellner finding is supportive, since hyperactivity is largely a male child problem.

Karlsson (1972) also showed that in a variety of play settings hyperactive children behaved like normal children. Following the same thread, Ellis, *et al.* (1971, 1973) showed in three studies that there were no detectable effects of a broad range of doses of methylphenidate on the informal play behavior of hyperactive children. These hyperactivity studies supported the notion that hyperactivity is a situational or contextual problem. Hyperactivity seemed only to appear in formal on-task settings. This argues strongly for modification of the setting rather than the tissue chemistry of the child, even though methylphenidate did not seem to have deleterious side-effects in the informal setting. It may be said that the efficiency of the drug buys time while the mechanisms governing hyperactivity and ways of managing it are sought.

The biorhythm studies of Ellis, Wade, and Bohrer (1970), and Wade, Ellis, and Bohrer (1973) demonstrated objectively that the often reported periodicities in children's play activity did exist. Two studies in very similar settings revealed a complex periodicity consisting of a short (about 15 minute) cycle superimposed on a long cycle (about 40 minutes). The cycles could be modified by environmental manipulation, suggesting that they are, in part, exogeneously driven. It was argued that two independent mechanisms, habituation/boredom and activity/rest, were the determinants of the periodicities.

Using a similar argument and method, Wade (1973) showed that institutionalized hyperkinetic children did not exhibit periodicities in their activity. They emitted a general low-level random behavior that supports the argument that the activity of hyperkinetics is driven by a quite different mechanism from that of hyperactivity.

On the opposite front Linford *et al.* (1971) confirmed that children exhibiting Down's Syndrome were hypoactive. When collaborating with Duthie (1970), he noted that their hypoactivity was not due to physiological limitations, since the children could work hard and maintain heart rates in excess of 180 beats per minute. Linford argued that his subjects had difficulty with the cognitive rather than physiological substrate of their play behavior.

Collectively, these studies point to the power of the environment to manipulate activity, and that the child × setting interaction is the arena for future research. Such internal concepts like surplus energy and minimal brain damage seem dangerously simplistic.

Supporting the theme which claims that the setting is an important determinant of activity is the large number of studies (Wuellner, 1965; Wade, Ellis, and Bohrer, 1971; Witt, 1971; and Scholtz and Ellis, 1974 reported in Chapter 3) that found that peers were the most important influence. Time and again the physical environment was modified, often quite drastically, and time and again the concurrent manipulations of the social setting ran away with the variance. It is time that our interest in designing for play be switched from concern for engineering the physical setting to understanding and managing the social matrix in which play usually takes place.

Chapter 5 | Boredom and Creativity

Introduction

The majority of the studies reported so far have involved the analysis of children playing in a free-range setting. This chapter reports studies that follow two themes in which children were asked, at least at the beginning of a session, to play in a particular way. The procedures in these studies were designed to focus the behavior of the child on a set of actions by means of instructions and procedures. In the first theme the task was a dummy task, and the experimenters were really interested in what the child's off-task behavior revealed about the human propensity to continue to emit apparently non-contingent behaviors. The second theme is knit together by the concept of creativity and the factors influencing creative production.

In the first theme the dummy task was used to reassure the children by giving their behavior a focus. All the children had become used to participating in learning experiments in which they were asked to perform in an experiment for a "friend" (an experimenter) and were often anxious if they were left alone in an experimental suite without a clear task assigned.

The tasks were always simple and completed quickly, thus leaving much empty time to be filled. The absence of externally applied consequences during much of an experimental session left internal consequences to drive the behavior most of the time. Thus, analysis of the behavior emitted after completion of the task itself was expected to reveal much about the intriguing behavior that is intrinsically, or at least not extrinsically, motivated.

The theoretical formulations dealt with in Chapter 2 and called either arousal seeking or information seeking came under more direct test in this set of studies. In all cases the studies aimed to vary the information inherent in the setting and predict the kinds of behaviors emitted by the children. In this series of studies the behavior of the children was usually video-taped and subject to a very fine-grained analysis using standardized observational procedures. In these studies the general predictions were that more information rich tasks or settings would sustain task related activities for longer, thus diminishing off-task behaviors.

Stereotyped Behavior

The first studies of this kind were conducted by Gramza (Gramza, 1974; Gramza and Reynolds, 1974) in which stereotyped behaviors in normal children were studied. Stereotyped behaviors have been an obvious and often damaging problem in the management of hyperkinetic children. Stereotyped behaviors are the rocking, head-banging, pacing, exaggerated grooming, and picking behaviors that render the behavior of institutionalized retardates and long-caged zoo animals so bizarre. These behaviors have been defined collectively as ". . . characterized by the frequent, almost mechanical, repetition of a posture or movement which varies only slightly in form from time to time, and which serves no obvious function (or goal)" (Davenport and Menzel, 1963).

Since Davenport and Menzel (1963) made their definitions there have been attempts to identify the cause or goal of the activity. Two explanations have surfaced.

The first explanation is built on the observation that stereotypies seem to occur in settings where there is perceptual deprivation and/or movement restraint. It has also been noted that the provision of material with impact or the opportunity to engage in alternate activities reduces stereotypies. Seen against the backdrop of the sensory restriction literature dealt with in Ellis (1973), and also in Chapter 2, stereotypies seem to be the responses made by an organism trapped in a setting with inadequate possibilities for the generation of information. Another way of saying this is that if play is information seeking activity, then stereotypies appear when an individual's opportunities for play are exhausted. Thus, stereotypies are the behaviors of an organism disorganized by perceptual deprivation. It has been argued that emitting stereotyped behaviors, and nulling the errors in them to maintain their form, require information processing. It is the information so produced that maintains these behaviors (Ellis, 1973). These behaviors, then, are the behaviors of last resort in the struggle to fill time in impoverished environments.

The second explanation is that the perceptual deprivation is stressful in itself. The negative affect engendered by perceptual deprivation rises with increased exposure to a constant setting and induces anxiety or supra-optimal arousal. Given this stressed state the organism learns to emit and attend to highly redundant activities that reduce the arousal level to tolerable levels. Thus, stereotyped behaviors are used as a procedure for reducing "tension" by providing familiar non-arousing stimulation to attend to.

These two explanations are in a sense equally useful. They are both hypothetical constructs that lie among the antecedent circumstances, chronic perceptual deprivation, and the emission of highly repetitious responses.

It may be that the two supposed mechanisms work additively. For example Kaufman and Levitt (1965) found that stereotypies increased in periods of presumed increasing general "tension" just prior to meals and periods of increased restriction (the rest periods). Also Hutt and Hutt (1965) found them to increase in autistic children placed in complex settings, and Levitt and Kaufman (1965) have elevated stereotypy levels by bombarding the children with irritating or tension inducing levels of white noise (85 db and 110 db).

There is no question, however, that stereotypies are undesirable both in the cage and the institution. The extant research suggests ways of managing the behavior. For example at about this time Hollis (1965) found that sterotypies were reduced in profoundly retarded children by housing them in situations containing many novel objects.

Stereotyped Behavior in Normal Children

Gramza (1974) was interested in testing the notion that some forms of stereotyped behavior were normal and could be controlled by environmental enrichment. These ideas had escaped those most troubled by the phenomenon. Program managers in institutions for the retarded usually blamed the nature of their charges for the problem rather than their own management procedures.

His first study had two phases. The first phase was to catalog the behaviors elicited in normal children by an extremely boring, or perceptually deprived, setting. He asked children to remain alone (for 4 minute periods) in a normally lit soundproof experimental suite with no manipulable materials except themselves and their clothes. The session was videotaped and careful analysis revealed that there were 30 categories into which the children's behavior fell (see Appendix AVII). Since there were no externally defined goals the repetition of these behaviors represented the degree to which behaviors became stereotyped.

The second stage involved testing the hypothesis that stereotypies in normal children increased with time spent in a constant and boring setting.

Gramza tested ten each of 4–5 year old boys and girls in a small (10 ft. ×
11 ft.) room in which there hung a board with colored Christmas tree lights.
The lights were controlled by acoustic frequency switches while music was
played to the children, resulting in a standardized pattern of flashing lights.
The board thus produced low level acoustic-visual display, which was held
constant throughout the study.

In this study the children were asked merely to stand in a square marked
on the carpet in range of the two video cameras and wait for the experimenter
for four minutes on each of two successive days. This task was not perceived
as a task by the children, and a few complained so vigorously at the unusual
absence of a task and the apparent aversiveness of an empty room that they
had to be returned to their classroom prior to finishing their vigil. Thus,
those who tolerated the experience were biased in the direction of tolerance
of boredom and provided a conservative test.

Despite the bias in the sample completing the test, the results were
simple and clear cut. For both boys and girls the number of sterotyped
responses increased dramatically across time, both within the four minute
trials and across the two days ($F = 108.46$ with 1 and 18 df, p $< .0001$ and
$F = 21.88$ with 1 and 18 df, p $< .0001$).

If entrapment for four minutes within a boring setting leads to an elevated stereotypy emission rate, and that rate is elevated on a second exposure,
it is not surprising that retardates who are trapped for years within the confines of their crowded and impoverished dayrooms develop bizarre behaviors.

Gramza and Reynolds went on to test the corollary of their first finding.
They wanted to know whether the sensory enrichment of the standardized
and aversively boring setting reduced the occurrence of stereotyped behaviors. They extended the first study in several ways. They increased the number
of tolerant subjects by adding a task that was perceived as a task by the children. The children were asked merely to wait for a three-note sound signal,
then press a button on an impressive looking box located in the corner of the
room, and return to their square. The box had dummy lights, etc. and was
labeled "Phlangle Box." It was designed to fit the children's expectations
that each experimental suite they visited would contain some kind of sophisticated psychological rig. The button-pressing signal consisted of three short
800 Hz tones every 30 seconds, while the children's activation of their button
produced short 3000 Hz tone.

While waiting in the square the child was exposed to the acoustic-visual
board that was programmed to have either a very low or a very high
complexity content. These two conditions were replicated once for each
child, thus producing four counterbalanced four minute exposures to the
settings.

Again videotapes of the 20 4 to 5-year-old boys and girls were used to
identify the number and content of the stereotyped behaviors emitted in the

setting. Inspection of the means revealed that fewer stereotypes occurred in the enriched setting (.838 versus .968) and on day 1 (.799 versus .986). Conventional analysis of stereotypy variance in this design was thwarted because of empty cells in the balanced design, but the means support the contention that stimulus deprivation leads to stereotyped behavior. However, no confidence level for these inferences was computed.

Causes of Stereotyped Behavior

These two simple studies confirmed the view that stereotypies arise in perceptually degraded and boring settings. The rapid increase in their incidence can be detected when using sophisticated observational procedures and should be considered a normal reaction to the deprivation. Further, Gramza and Reynolds showed quite simply that enriching the environment suppressed the incidence and delayed the onset of stereotypies. While neither study cleared up which of two, or the combination of two, intervening mechanisms drove the behavior, they clearly pointed the finger at the role modulation of the environment had to play in generating, maintaining, and presumably eventually elaborating, stereotyped behaviors in children.

Boredom and Information Seeking

The third study in this series was conducted by Barnett (1974) and involved children in the completion of two jigsaw like puzzles (see Figure 5.1). While both puzzles were simple, one was far simpler than the other. The puzzles were varied to alter the amount of uncertainty within

SIMPLE PUZZLES

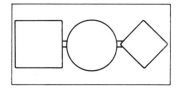 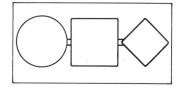

COMPLEX PUZZLES

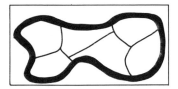 

Fig. 5.1: Diagram of the two simple and complex puzzles used in the boredom and information seeking study by Barnett (1974).

them. Thus the children were dealing with tasks that varied in the information contained in them so that hypotheses concerning their on-task and off-task behavior could be tested.

Barnett argued that information-seeking behavior was modulated by the need to maintain arousal level. She argued that children were, in effect, an information channel with a given optimal capacity to process information, and they acted to maintain their own idiosyncratic rate of information flow. Since familiar objects and settings contained little information, children would respond to simple and redundant settings by generating information. She cited Berlyne for the kinds of overt behavior emitted to produce information: exploration, investigation, and manipulation.

Children were expected to move through stages when pursuing information. First they explored for an opportunity to engage with the environment and generate information. Upon coming across such an opportunity the children probed and investigated the properties of the object or setting. After this the task's perceived task demands were satisfied. At this point the children were expected to proceed to a phase in which they either played with the object and setting, using it in a variety of new ways to generate information, or passed on and explored further in order to begin the stages again with a new source of information.

By videotaping and carefully categorizing the overt behaviors of the children playing with these puzzles, Barnett hoped to test several hypotheses derived from the information-seeking model. She expected that with repeated exposure, investigatory and manipulatory behavior would decrease and be replaced by more novel off-task behaviors as the children sought to generate interesting responses. These expectations were then refined to predict the different behaviors emitted with the complex rather than the simple puzzle. The complex puzzle, because of its higher information content, was expected to sustain more task related behaviors. There would be less off-task behaviors and more investigatory and manipulatory behaviors. After completion the children also were expected to return to the complex task more often than to the simple task.

The study used 11 boys and 14 girls, between the ages of 4.33 and 5.25 ($\overline{X} = 4.77$) years, who were randomly selected from the Children's Research Center Nursery School. The children were divided into four groups. Each group attended twice and received one of the four possible permutations:

Simple—Simple
Simple—Complex
Complex—Simple
Complex—Complex

The children's behavior was broken down into categories that logically related to its information-gathering aspects. The first set of behaviors related to the task and were classified as on-task behaviors (operational definitions are listed in Appendix AVIII). They were Investigation, Investigation/

Manipulation and Execution. The next set involved off-task behaviors and were called Procedural Off-tasks and Miscellaneous Off-tasks. They captured responses not directly associated with the task like fidgeting, looking around the room, fiddling with apparatus, and behaviors required by the procedures. The final set of responses followed the first completion of the puzzle. They included novel on-task responses in which the child created new ways of dealing with the puzzle (NOVONTS), novel responses to other elements in the environment (NOVOFFTS), and repetitive solving of the puzzle (OLDONTS).

Having broken the total behavior down into the categories, the time in each was expressed as a proportion of the total and transformed (arcsine square root) to allow for parametric analysis. Each variable was subjected to variance analysis using a simple linear model to determine the reliability of the differences necessary to test the hypotheses.

The first hypothesis concerned the behavior from the start of the session to completion of the puzzle for the first time. It was expected that the higher complexity puzzle would require more investigation and manipulation than the simple toy, and that these behaviors would both diminish on the second exposure.

The analysis (reported in great detail in Barnett, 1974) revealed that children indeed spent more time investigating and manipulating the complex puzzle ($F = 23.4$ with 1 and 20 df. $p \leq .001$), but there was only a suggestion in the means that this time was reduced with exposure. This is not a particularly important finding because, not only did the complex puzzle contain more information in the cognitive sense, but there was also more information in the actual motor responses necessary to fit the puzzle together. In fact since the time taken to manipulate and solve the puzzle was only marginally reduced with practice, it seems that manipulation time was limited by the time it took to physically move the more complex pieces into place.

The second hypothesis involved off-task behavior. Since the simple puzzle made very limited demands on the child it was expected that, when given this puzzle, the child would generate more responses involving the setting. Although the means tended to support this assertion there were no statistically significant effects on these variables.

The third hypothesis argued that the complex puzzle was difficult to complete and would sustain repeated solution. However, the simple puzzle would engender more novel and creative responses once it had been solved. In other words the children would be forced to go beyond the task.

The data support this notion. The group given the simple puzzle produced more novel responses involving the task ($F = 7.2$ with 1×20 df. $p < .025$). All children produced more novel off-task behaviors on the second session ($F = 7.7$ with 1×20 df. $p < .025$).

The appearance of novel on-task behaviors and novel off-task responses (creative responses involving the puzzle and the setting) increased across sessions for all groups but one. It was expected that the children experiencing the same puzzle in both sessions (simple-simple; complex-complex) would increase their playful behavior in the second session; the challenge of the puzzle being exhausted in the initial session. The group moving from the complex to the simple puzzle should be more playful in the second session because the novelty of the task and setting and the complexity of the task were both reduced on the second session. The remaining children, those who moved from the simple to complex puzzle, *reduced* the playfulness of their behaviors in the second session. These children generated some novel behaviors during their first session after exhausting the information in the simple toy, as expected. However, the number of novel or playful behaviors was preempted when a more interesting puzzle was presented. These findings were reliable ($F = 2.57$ and 7.76, df 1 and 23, p $< .025$, for novel on-task and novel off-task responses, respectively).

Taken together, the findings of this study support the assertion that once the children had exhausted the information in the puzzle, they turned to the other items in the setting.

Barnett also collected heart rate data although that was not reported. In the analyses of heart rate, no patterns were found that consistently and logically related to the behavior categories when the data were analysed by toys, or their qualities, or even by days.

This Barnett study demonstrates that when the information is not directly available in a task, the children will turn to an engagement with the setting and finally will produce their most creative responding as a strategy for adding information by transforming the functions of the materials available. Thus the most playful behavior occurred when the task demands of a task in a setting were exhausted—an assertion made previously by Sutton-Smith (1973) and by Scholtz and Ellis (1975a).

This Barnett study was the first fine-grain analysis of the play of single children that was carried to a successful conclusion. It was the precursor of further studies that were organized quite differently and were not successful. Since science should proceed from the examination of studies that do not work well in addition to those that do, the remaining two studies will be briefly dealt with, together with the lessons to be learned.

Physiological Correlates of Play

The three studies (Ellis, Barnett, and Korb, 1973; Barnett, 1974; Barnett, Ellis, and Korb, 1974) were all concerned with the correlation of internal biological events with overt behaviors. The studies were designed to detect the psycho-physiological correlates of play behavior. It was hypothesized that information seeking was modulated by an arousal mechanism that would, in turn, modulate various psycho-physiological measures. It was hoped to observe the arousal mechanism in action. If this were possible then a dazzling new vista for the behavioral sciences would open up. The playful mode of responding would be measurable directly, not by observation of the response, but by changes in the indicators of the central state of the subject.

The first study argued that, as the child moved through a stream of responses with a play object, the arousal level would vary with the rate of information flow. Thus during investigation of a novel object, arousal would be high. When information was exhausted the child would pass on to manipulations, and finally, when the information in the possible interactions were exhausted, the child would reject the toy and emit new responses elevating the level of information. Thus it was expected that, by measuring the level of psycho-physiological arousal during a stream of responses, we would see an interrelation between modifications of the responses emitted and the central state. We hoped to see the child's behavior modifying the arousal level and then, vice versa, in a dynamic interplay.

The first study presented five toys that were presumed to vary in the information they presented. Some toys had obvious task demands that would require little investigation. Some of the toys also presented more manipulative opportunities. These qualities of the toys were varied independently although with five toys the variations were not completely balanced. Nevertheless these qualities were identified beforehand, and their variation in the two attributes was expected to modify the kinds of information carried by the toys and the way the children played with them.

The toys were hidden in six easily reached boxes (one box contained no toy as a control for the information inherent in just operating a box). The children were asked to play with a toy until they were finished with it and then place it in a bin. This act would release another toy, and the order of presentation was randomized. All boxes were wired so that each new set of operations was event-marked on a polygram.

The output from a cardiotachometer and the galvanic skin resistance was recorded simultaneously, and the videotape was made of the split images of the children and the setting and a millisecond counter. Thus all events were very accurately time-locked together. From the analysis of the time-related changes in behavior and internal events we expected to test the different effects of the qualities of the toys on the behavior and on the psycho-physiological measures, and to predict the rejection of the toy in favor of a new toy from antecedent psycho-physiological events.

Technical, procedural, and analytical problems soon reared their heads. Baseline drifts in GSR required on-line adjustments of the record to center the pen; sensitivity of the GSR to the children's movements; and unpredictable, but necessary, alterations in sensitivity during a session made analysis of the GSR trace extremely difficult. The lack of resolution in the cardio-tachogram meant it had to be completely rejected.

Procedural problems arose because the children were overwhelmed by the complex procedure, and most spent their time satisfying it, rather than playing with the toys. It was an experimenter's, not a child's, set-up, and the children were nervous and tried too hard to do what they thought we wanted. This was compounded by the fact that the toys were not as interesting as the procedures, so that the children moved rapidly through the experiment without playing very much with individual toys. Because of the existence of other toys in other boxes in the set-up, it was like Christmas morning with children rapidly rejecting the current toy and rushing on to the next.

Concerns for the validity and reliability of the dependent variables and the confusions introduced by the children's being required to make complex responses stimulated another attempt.

In the second experiment a more recently discovered indicator of interest and attention, or higher processing of information, was used. It was heart-rate variance (Porges and Raskin, 1969). Heart-rate variance had been shown to diminish when the subject was actively attending to a stimulus array and was presumably a physiological concomitant of the activation of the central nervous system required to process information. This indicator seemed to be exactly what was necessary to reveal the internal events that accompany play behavior, given that it is the behavior that is instrumental in generating information.

The previous experiments had allowed the children too much latitude, and the movements associated with their play had confused the picture. In this experiment it was decided to purge the experiment of as much motor behavior as possible, and to simplify the display. Thus two displays were used. One was a set of clips from color cartoon films showing a behavior and its consequence (Yogi bear hits ranger and runs away). Each clip lasted about 20 seconds. The second and simple condition consisted of a set of black and white clips of a white square or circle or triangle moving slowly onto, about, and off a black background. Only one figure appeared at a time. In both displays it was possible to leave the loop running and repeat the display at either the child's or the experimenter's discretion.

The children were seated in a dimly lit experimental room empty except for chair and screen. There were no sources of information except the display because the room was highly familiar.

Under the initial condition the subjects were allowed to control their own information flow by switching film clips from one display to the other. It was expected that the oscillations in heart-rate variance would be small because the subjects had the wherewithal to track their own central value for the heart-rate variance. In the contrasting condition, the subjects were alternately trapped—60-second bouts with the highly redundant and 60-second bouts with the information-rich displays. Under these conditions the heart-rate variance was expected to oscillate reliably under the control of the experimenter.

The analysis of this data was to proceed in two stages, and only one stage had been completed at the time of writing. In the first stage the durations spent with the complex and simple loops by the subjects free to control the display were analysed. Here the dependent variables were complex. First the traces were divided into eight 60-second segments to allow for eventual comparison with the traces produced when children were automatically switched every 60 seconds. Then the duration spent on the simple and complex loops within that minute was computed and divided by session length to convert to proportions, which in turn were normalized by Arcsine square root transformation. As expected the children spent more time with the complex display throughout the session. ($p < .0001$).

The values of this duration variable for both simple and complex levels were not independent. If more time is spent with the complex display, then less time is spent with the simple. This dependency was removed by dividing the duration scores for each complexity level by the number of changes. Thus, the duration spent on each selection of a complex or simple loop could vary independently from the other.

Children spent significantly longer time with the complex loop on average ($p < .0001$). However, the mean durations were not uniformly different. After one minute the children spent as much time with the simple display as with the complex display (see Figure 5:2). It was as if having formed expectations for the complex loop and finding it familiar they switched attention to the simple loop to search for information there. Finding it highly redundant, preference was switched to the cartoon display. The time spent on the cartoon loops mirrored this, but during the last minute or so they began to lose their hold on the children. Although this interaction only approached significance ($p \leq .18$) the trends are interesting and in line with other findings. It is as if the children responded immediately to the obvious on-task content (complex > simple), then searched for an alternative (durations converge in minute 2), then settled into a preference for the complex display for the next four minutes (complex > simple) and then in the last two minutes even the complex displays became sufficiently redundant for them to lose their attractiveness. Since the children did not spend a compensatory increase in time with the simple loop, they were probably beginning to search elsewhere for information. The drop probably heralds the beginning of off-task responding and developing aversion to the setting. This is speculation and needs a longer experiment and off-task behavior measures to check.

The findings to date are not surprising, and the more interesting analyses of the psycho-physiological correlates and the comparisons of the sessions paced by the experimenter and by the children themselves are still pending.

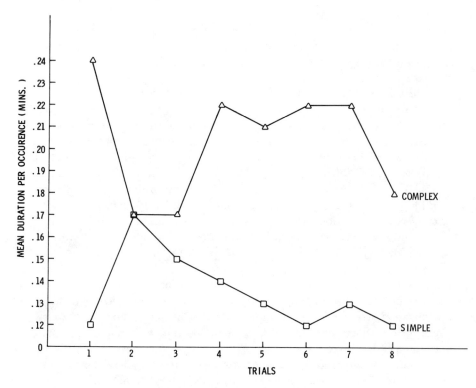

Fig. 5.2: Effects of the complexity of the film loops on children's preferences for them.

However, inspection suggests that the individual psycho-physiological data do not look promising.

These studies were searching for central state correlates of overt behavior. While the analyses of the overt behaviors are highly consistent with the other studies of similar behaviors, the analyses of the central state measures were frustrating. They found evidence neither for, nor against, the hypotheses. The experiments bogged down in technical and analytical problems. These studies have not been carried to a conclusion and await either the acquisition of new scientific skills by the experimenters, the attention of psycho-physiologists, or the development of new and more robust indicators of arousal.

Development of Creativity

For the remainder of this chapter we turn to studies that tried to shed light on the development of creativity in children. Clearly, mankind faces a baffling array of problems both personally and as a species. The enhancement of individual and group capacities to deal creatively with extant problems is important. This notion is underlined by Torrance (1965):

> As we studied creative behavior among both children and adults it became increasingly clear that perhaps nothing could contribute more to the general welfare of our nation and the satisfaction and mental health of the people than a general raising of the level of creative behavior.

Raising the level of creativity in the population requires a clear understanding of the processes whereby creativity is developed and expressed. The three studies that follow were motivated by the need to contribute to this understanding. All three studies involved young children and probed the relations between the play of children and their creativity.

The first study was conducted by Bishop and Chace (1971). They separated creative production from potential creativity. Creative production is the result of cognitive activity that is focused on a problem in order to produce novel or unique solutions. In this context the "problem" may not be crucial to the survival of the individual nor even practical but involves a question to which an answer or answers are sought. Thus creative production results from epistemic behavior. In estimating creative production, it is necessary to separate novelty from utility. To move from an idea to a practical reality may require the special skills and resources of others. While some tend to downplay the flights of fancy of the creative person, the creative idea has primacy; without it the disposition of resources to implement a solution cannot begin.

Potential creativity can only be inferred from creative production. It is a label for those dispositions and behaviors that allow a person to produce relatively novel or creative responses. Potential creativity, or capacity to produce creativity, is presumed to vary among individuals.

Effect of Rearing Patterns

Given that potential creativity varies among individuals and that its enhancement is important, then understanding the processes that increase it becomes crucial. Once again recognizing that at this time we cannot interfere with the germ plasm and can only manipulate experiences, the question becomes; "What rearing experiences enhance the potential creativity of children?" Bishop and Chace (1971) attempted to answer this question by studying the way one aspect of each of the children's rearing environment influenced his or her potential creativity. They studied factors influencing the play settings of each child and observed the effect on the child's creative production.

The play environment of each child was chosen for study because many workers have claimed that opportunities for playful engagement with the world enhance creative potential (Greenacre, 1959; Torrance, 1964; Lieberman, 1965; Sutton-Smith, 1967). The principles underlying the interrelation are simple. When playful, the child is freed from external consequences for each response. Thus responses can be made for their own sake without fear of error. The stimulation-seeking model predicts that when so freed, the press for stimuli exhibiting collative properties will reward novel and surprising responses. As a result playful settings encourage novel, flexible, and unique responses. Such responses are the stuff of creative production. If children are often allowed by the social and physical setting to behave "playfully" then a playful mode of responding will be practised; and potential creativity will be enhanced.

Bishop and Chace argued that a most powerful determinant of children's rearing environment influencing playful behaviors was the conceptual structure of the parents. Parents who are dogmatic, rule, or precedent oriented are unlikely to support creative production in their children. Their rules for governing family life are likely to be restrictive, and their provisions for play are likely to be less flexible than those of parents at the other pole. Parents who are not rule-dependent but have a flexible and abstract conceptual style are more likely to encourage and provide for playful behavior. Thus, Bishop and Chace postulated that parents ordered along a concrete-abstract continuum will be consistent in their influences on the play environment that will influence their children's creative potential.

Bishop and Chace studied 72 children, their parents, and their home environment. They ordered the parents along the conceptual continuum using Harvey's (1963, 1966) technique. This involved filling out a booklet in which they were asked their beliefs about ten issues. These statements were then independently rated by four judges and placed into four categories from strongly concretistic dependent thinking to highly abstract interdependent answers. When three judges agreed, the data was accepted.

After filling out the "This I believe . . ." test, two questionnaires, the first dealt with each parent's attitudes to play, rights of children, relations to adults, etc. The second dealt with factual descriptions of the home play environment and was given to the mother. (It seems that all the caring ones in this sample were the children's mothers.)

The final link in the chain was to assess the potential creativity of the children by objectively testing their creative production. To do this Bishop and Chace developed a test that allowed many different estimates of flexibility and preference for complexity to be generated simultaneously. They asked children to select random shapes from a board and make anything they wanted on an identical but empty response board. The boards were separated so that a response was clearly identifiable. The nine shapes had different numbers of inflexion points (3 equilateral triangles, 3 obtuse triangles; 4; 6; 8; 12; 16; 20; 24) and were arranged in order. These were six rows, each of a different color, and the left-right arrangements were counterbalanced.

From observation the order of choice was recorded, and from a color photograph of the product of 2-minute session six dependent variables were derived.

The dependent variables assessed different aspects of the tendency to avoid predictable patterns. They were: complexity of chosen shapes, variation in color choice, variation in shape, combined variation of color and shape, and variation in sequence (See Appendix AIX).

Bishop and Chace now had data on parental conceptual systems, their beliefs about play, their actual provisions for play at home, and a variety of indices of the creative production of their children. The division of the parents into abstract or concrete thinkers was used as the independent variable, and its effect on the various dependent variables describing home environment and creative production was analyzed.

Analysis of these sets of data eliminated fathers from contention as a determinant of their children's potential creativity. Mothers, however, presumably by the weight of their consistent presence and influence, produced a different story. There were 45 mothers who could be classified reliably according to Harvey (1966), and they were pooled into two classifications—concrete and abstract thinkers.

These two groups of mothers held significantly different opinions about their children's play. They disagreed on the followed rephrased statements.

Children should be seen and not heard.
Boys/girls should be discouraged from playing with girls/boys, toys, and games.
Adults should play with their children.
Wrestling or rough housing should be done only outdoors or in designated areas.
When a child is using a toy incorrectly, the parent should stop and teach the correct way.

More abstract thinking mothers reliably adopted a position that was consistent with engendering playfulness in their children. When the factual questionnaire was analyzed further clear differences between concrete versus abstract thinking mothers surfaced.

On 10 of the 12 statements in the Home Play Environment questionnaire there were reliable differences in the actual conditions supporting play in the home. Edited versions of these statements follow:

Does child have own record player?
Does child sing or dance along with music?
Is child allowed to use adult items and equipment?
How often does child use non-commercial playthings?
How often has parent helped make or made play things?
Under what conditions are playthings made? With only parental advice, help, instruction?
How often do you teach new games or new ways to play old ones?

How often do you play with child according to rules or games devised by him?

On a given occasion how long does a play session with your child last?

Bishop and Chace (1971) deal with these questions in detail, but summarize by saying that,

> Conceptually more abstract parents provide their children with play environments that are more playful (perhaps because of the environments' greater complexity, autonomy for the child, and openness to new experiences). The remaining question is whether the children of more abstract parents behave in a way that can be regarded as more potentially creative (p. 330).

Table 5.1 presents the data on the creative performance of the children according to the conceptual development of their mothers. Of the six indexes of creative production three showed reliable differences and one marginal

Table 5.1

MEAN PERFORMANCE SCORES OF THE CHILDREN OF MOTHERS DIFFERING IN CONCEPTUAL DEVELOPMENT

Variable	$N = 13$ Concrete Mothers	$N = 15$ Abstract Mothers	$N = 17$ Abstract Mothers	t[a]	$P \leq$
(1) Relative complexity (No. of 3, 3, 4 pt—No. of 16, 20, 24 pt)	5.7	−2.3	−3.4	3.07	.005
(2) Mean Number of Inflection Points	6.7	9.2	8.2	−1.93	.05
(3) Relative Variation in Choice of Color	0.38	0.24	0.16	1.44	.05
(4) Relative Variation in Choice of Shape	0.38	0.42	0.27	.30	NS
(5) Relative Variation in Color and Shape	0.94	1.07	1.27	−.55	NS
(6) Sequential Variation in Choices	7.3	9.4	13.2	−2.10	.025

[a]The t test compared the combined mean score of the children of abstract mothers to that of children of concrete mothers. Note that "abstract" refers to mothers classified as stage 3 and stage 4, and "concrete" as stage 1, in Harvey's (1963) classification.

From Bishop and Chace (1971).

reliability. Thus children of more abstract thinking mothers "chose more complex figures, used a greater variety of colours, and obtained their final set of figures through a more complex and varied choice sequence (i.e. . . . showed an increasing tendency to shift from different columns and rows of the stimulus board from choice N to choice N + 1)" (Bishop and Chace, 1971, p. 335).

Since the parents exhibiting the different conceptual systems did not differ with respect to age, education, income, or class, the original hypotheses were supported, with the refinement that it should be applied to mothers. Mothers classified as more abstract according to Harvey's criteria (1963) reported that the environments in which their children played were more flexible, exploratory, and autonomous. These conditions suggest a playful environment, and children reared in such an environment were more likely to emit complex and varied behaviors in a laboratory task designed to facilitate and measure creative production.

It seems reasonable to account for the lack of a "father effect" in the data by assuming that it was the mothers who were the partners involved in rearing. They were in contact with their children, and it was their conceptual system that most clearly influenced the environment and behavior of their children. Thus it was the mother's interactions with the child that modified the creative potential of the child.

This paper contributed to a growing body of evidence that organisms reared in restricted settings have reduced capacity to deal with novelty both in received stimuli and expressed responses. It seems clear that this paper is in line with the claims of Sutton-Smith (1967) that a restrictive home environment restricts not only the child's range of potential responses, but also the child's potential preference for novel stimuli.

Effect of Rearing Patterns in Preschool

Continuing from Bishop and Chace, Banks (1973) argued that if mothers influenced their children's play environment and presumably eventually influenced their potential creativity, then so should preschool teachers. Banks suggested that the influences of the conceptual systems of parent and teacher should interact additively.

Banks studied 80 children, their parents, and the four teachers from the same pre-school that was used by Bishop and Chace. He gave the same "This I believe" test to parents and teachers and added Harvey's (1971) Teacher Rating Scale. He also administered the home play environment questionnaire, and derived 13 measures of creative production from: 1) The Bishop and Chace (1971) Complexity Board test, 2) Thinking Creatively with Pictures, Form A (Torrance, 1966), 3) Banks' Play Behavior Test (1973, See Appendix AX). Banks tested the additive effects of parental and teacher conceptual development on the environmental variables and on the 13 dependent variables using the interactions in a multivariate analysis of variance (MANOVA).

The results were not clear-cut. When the parents' conceptual systems were in agreement, then creativity was enhanced. Thus, having two concrete thinking parents or two abstract thinkers enhanced creativity ($F = 2.19$, df 13 and 47. $p \leq .025$). When taken in combination and allowing for their intercorrelation, it was possible to distinguish the interactive effects of the mother and father. Univariate tests revealed that on only one variable, the Banks Test estimate of flexibility, was there a significant effect. There were no effects due to teacher, and Banks suggests that these results be ascribed to chance.

The analysis of the home rearing environment also did not provide clear insights. Although some effects were significant, there was no consistent pattern of findings suggesting that the findings were important.

This study did not replicate others' findings. However, it was weak in the sense that it only studied four teachers, who worked in pairs. So in this study the possible interaction between parent and teacher was confounded by teacher/teacher interaction. Only if like teachers were paired could a teacher effect be expected. Obviously a much larger number of teachers should be studied. Finally, the *ex post facto* nature of this study, as always, allows a host of rival explanations. So this study is notable only for the idea. The notion of studying the interacting effects of the caring ones, mothers and fathers and teachers, is an important one. It remains to be seen whether they jointly influence creativity.

Rewarding Creativity

The following creativity experiment turned away from studying long term effects of facilitating or constricting playfulness. Bishop and Chace had stayed close at home and studied parents. They found that only mothers were an influence. Banks, on the trail of an interactive effect of parents and teachers on creativity, had found that the trails had petered out. On the assumption that the Banks study would be successful Reynold's and Ellis (1974) changed tracks and examined the immediate effects of reinforcing creativity in children. Simply put, they asked whether contingent social reinforcement that contained information revealing the contingency ("I like that because it's different.") would influence the creative production of children.

Reynolds and Ellis perceived the same link between play and creativity. Playful behavior occurred when consequences attached to criterion responses were removed. Thus, playfulness was presumed to flourish when many responses were permissible. Reynolds argued that if playfulness, and the creativity that seemed to result, was desired, then merely allowing any response might not be as powerful as actively rewarded responses that were creative; novel, fluent, flexible, and unique, to use Torrance's definitions of the ingredients of creative production. Thus Reynolds and Ellis wished to test the assumption that the attachment of reinforcements to the creative attributes of a response, rather than the response itself, would alter behavior towards increased creativity.

Pryor, Haag, and O'Reilly (1957), had convincingly demonstrated that a conservative dolphin had rapidly learned to emit responses that it had never emitted before. If a dolphin could learn to emit novel responses, then could children's level of creative production be modulated by social reinforcement by other humans? Thus, Reynolds and Ellis accepted the idea that other humans of differing conceptual systems influenced creativity on the one hand by altering the physical environment and on the other by altering the rules for behavior. They argued in addition that some parents are likely to reinforce playfulness and that social reinforcement was the most convenient mode. Demonstrating that creative production could be manipulated by social reinforcement was an important additional step in understanding the processes whereby creativity is enhanced and stabilized in children.

In addition to the simple question, "Does social reinforcement modulate creative production?", Reynolds and Ellis (1974) could not resist adding a theoretical wrinkle. Those researchers concerned with the mechanisms whereby social reinforcement functions can be divided into two schools: those who assert that the social reinforcement itself is rewarding, and the other school who contend that the reinforcement is effective because of the information it provides the subject about the response. Both arguments allow for learning and are usually confounded, thus allowing the argument to continue. For a review of this literature see Reynolds (1973).

While setting up the creativity experiment Reynolds and Ellis also separated the effect of the presence of a social reinforcer from the information it contained. For example, rewarding a child completing a step in a creative production task with the statement, "You're good at this!" presents only assent words, whereas, "I like that because it is different!" provides assent and the reason for it.

To answer the two questions required two pairs of groups and an extra group each experiencing a different treatment. In one pair, all the social reinforcements or responses contained information. In one group the rewarding responses were given when each of the children finished the production of a play object from play blocks and labeled it. In the paired group, each child received exactly the same reinforcements at exactly the same intervals as a child in the first group. So they received an identical number of rewards and information, but the rewards were not contingent on their production. In other words, the reinforcements were yoked from one group to the other.

The second pair of groups repeated this, but the praise statements did not contain information.

The fifth group acted as a control for the number of reinforcements and was allowed to continue until they had received the same number of reinforcements as a child receiving the contingent information-bearing statements.

The children, 38 males and 37 females ranging from 3–5 years were asked to build anything they wanted from several pairs of wooden blocks varying in size and shape, including rectangular, cylindrical, crescent and triangular configurations. They played in a small semi-circular booth and were told they could use all 14 blocks, but did not have to. When the children indicated they had finished, they were asked to label the object ("What is it?"; "Can you give it a name?"). The sessions were videotaped and lasted for eight minutes.

From the videotape five dependent variables were produced. They were fluency, flexibility, uniqueness, total number of responses, and number of blocks used (See Appendix AXI). Since only a few of the contrasts were required, and since the variables were moderately intercorrelated, multi-variate procedures were used. The complex analysis and results are reported in full elsewhere (Reynolds, 1973; Reynolds and Ellis, 1974). However, here the results can best be presented by listing them before their collective inter-pretation.

(1) The fluency and number of blocks used by the groups receiving information was significantly greater than that of the group receiving a yoked schedule of praise statements. ($F = 4.94$, df 1.55, p $<$ .03; and $F = 4.29$, df 1.55, p $<$ .04 respectively). Thus children who were told why they were praised and received the praise indirectly following the labeling a construction differently produced more objects and used more blocks in each of them.

(2) The groups receiving contingent praise produced objects with more blocks per construction and labeled them more flexibly than the group who received a yoked schedule of noncontingent statements ($F = 3.27$, df 1.55, p $<$ .08; $F = 3.24$, df 1.55, p $<$ .08 respectively). Therefore children who were praised directly after assigning a different label to a block construction used more blocks and produced more flexible labels than those receiving apparently random praise.

(3) A further set of tests was made to see whether a group who received as many praise statements as their paired subjects in the group given contingent information behaved differently. To allow for this the time spent playing had to be allowed to vary to hold the number of reinforcements constant. This contrast produced a significant multivariate ($F = 12.71$, df 1.55, p $<$ .0008). Further analysis revealed that the untimed contingent praise group were more fluent, more flexible, and had a higher rate of production than those given information. This means that children who were contingently rein-forced but denied information and not held to eight minutes were creatively the more productive.

The results of these contrasts can be integrated into an interesting descrip-tion of the strategies used by the children. The first composite effect revealed a strategy involving the number of blocks used. Those in the apparently random praise conditions used fewer blocks than those in the contingent condi-tions. It seems that there was a set to use all the blocks. Those who received praise when they had finished their construction, tended to use more blocks than those interrupted by a reinforcement in the process of building. Thus the non-contingently reinforced subjects, having utilized fewer blocks at the time they were reinforced, superstititously continued to produce using fewer blocks.

The increased fluency and reduced flexibility in the information group indicated another response strategy. The children who were told immediately why they had been praised seemed to adopt the most efficient strategy for generating further rewards. These children had high rates of production, but each of the objects tended to fall in the same category. Thus these children tended merely to modify the object and the label thus qualifying for reinforcement. This tactic increased the rate of production and reinforcement, but did not increase the flexibility or diversity of their production. On the other hand the group who were not given information but were allowed to produce as many objects (e.g. their time was not limited) were more flexible. The increase in flexibility seemed to be generated by a different strategy. The children receiving contingent praise were aware that completed and labeled objects resulted in praise, but they did not know why as the criterion was not available to them. They adopted a strategy of varying their responses, possibly in search for the connection, and they were more flexible. Those in the information group became complacent churning out more, but similar, responses.

This study points to the efficacy of the law of effect being applied to the attributes of a response and to its variability, rather than its mere occurrence. However, it also reveals the fragility of the creative response. Since the children were trying to maximize the rate of social reinforcement, they behaved consistently. Those given the key to the contingency, efficiently produced the consequences at the cost of reduced flexibility. Those who were denied the criterion tended to search for it and were more flexible as a result. This study exemplifies the complexity of the creative process and shows how easy it is to subvert the creative process by attaching external consequences to it.

Summary

This chapter has provided further evidence that the natural state of the human is not quiescence. When external consequences are removed behavior continues. Since work is defined as the behavior controlled by external consequences, the behavior that fills the vacuum has been called play; the simplistic opposite of work. In the first set of studies reported in this chapter the children were required to stay in a setting after some behaviors had satisfied the consequences implicit in complying with a set of instructions. After working at the task the children then turned to other behaviors. They manipulated themselves through stereotyped behaviors, the environment, exploration, or turned back to the task to emit novel task-related behaviors. They never sat or stood still waiting for the next criterion behavior to be called.

The link to creative responding is provided by the observation that when free of external consequences, the child often took the existing materials that had just been used to satisfy an external contingency and used them in a new way. These new responses seem rooted in the information-seeking process. The asking and answering of new questions about old materials, or the exploration of the environment for opportunities to interact, seems to be the root of the creative process. The central result of the information-seeking process must be an extension beyond the currently perceived limits of what is known and possible.

There seems to be a fundamental process that reinforces the playful extension of each human's reach into the world. This process has been stabilized by the exigencies of biological selection. The humans, and other animals, that were curious and creative, tended to survive. The expression of this curiosity and creativity seems to be influenced by rearing conditions. Mothers, at least, seem to have a generalized effect on the expressed creativity of their children. This may be because of the development in the child of a set of expectancies concerning likely adult reception of novel and creative responses, a familiarity with more complex and curious material and its use, or the development of strategies for generating behavior that extracts novelty, complexity, and flexibility from common materials in the environment. Alternatively, and more likely, the rearing conditions influence all these, and they interact to influence the potential a child has to be creative in any setting.

Finally, it was neatly demonstrated by Reynolds that the attachment of any consequences, beyond that of a general social support for the creative process, subverted it, something that artists have been telling us for a long time.

Chapter 6 | Review and Preview

This chapter summarizes the work so far by taking the body of research as a whole and trying to say succinctly what it means. This chapter stands like the period at the end of a sentence. It closes off what has just taken place, and prepares the reader for what comes next. It starts with the obvious failures, and in order to finish on a positive note, reviews the successes and points into the future.

Failures

There were two hardware failures. The first was the telepedometer which was fun for the engineers, but in its completed form, was of little use to the researchers. It may still have potential as an idea for measuring locomotor activity in another setting, but it will have to be thought through again.

The second hardware failure was the helmet device. It was developed to measure the oxygen consumption in the free range as unobtrusively as possible in order to calibrate the trace from the heart-rate telemetry device directly to energy expenditure. It was hoped to use it to calibrate the energy expenditure of individual children via estimates of the oxygen consumed per heart beat. Many of the hardware problems in the helmet were on their way to solution by the time the third prototype had been built. However, funding difficulties prevented further progress.

The next failure was well documented in Chapter 5 and was the frustrating experience of having a timely idea and being unable to test it. The idea involved a test of the information or arousal seeking formulation by correlating two resultants of the internal playful cognitive event; the overt acts and the covert psycho-physiological events accompanying the hypothesized change in arousal. The problem resided in being unable to find and record a meaningful indicator of central level of arousal with our limited resources. So, although the information seeking formulation is consistent with much of the observed behavior of children, we have not yet directly demonstrated the intervening arousal seeking mechanism.

A further failure is one shared by the behavioral sciences in general. Frequently, the exigencies of a theory and the real world forced the design of an experiment that went beyond the reach of contemporary statistics. Once our research reached the level of making multivariate tests of hypotheses the trouble began. We found that appropriate *post-hoc* tests and estimates of power had not yet been worked out for the multivariate mode. Also our questions concerning the limits of the theoretical assumptions of normality, homogeneity of variance in variance analyses, homogeneity and the linearity of regression in covariance analyses, together with the practical problems of forming solutions for unbalanced and irregular designs, caused our statistician friends to throw up their hands and claim that, "That isn't known yet." These limitations emphasize the need for increased and sustained funding of applied statisticians. In our case, our vision of the research often exceeded the reach of contemporary statistical analysis.

Successes

One legacy of the work reported here is the armament of new dependent variables suitable for the study of play and play related behaviors, both in the free range and in constrained settings.

The free-range variables exploited new technologies unavailable to the workers who began the study of children in play areas back in the nineteen thirties. The utilization of the fish-eye camera system was a simple and useful advance that was rendered more powerful by the development of computer software to generate many dependent variables exploiting the camera's capacity to fix the position of children in time and space. The system was used in many studies and was shown to be highly reliable. Since neither the hardware nor software was treated in Hutt and Hutt's (1970) recent survey of observational methods, they have been treated in considerable detail in the text and appendices.

Parallel to the work that developed the photographic system were other efforts to capture "activity" by the transduction of some of the energy associated with it or by the use of physiological changes associated with the expenditure of energy. One such system was successful.

The successful system was the multi-channel heart rate telemetry system. The processes involved in developing multiple telemetry were not, of course, developed in our laboratory. Well-known principles were merely applied to the production of a child-proof telemetry system. While this involved only creative engineering to radio-telemeter a signal triggered by a child's heartbeats, it provided the base from which another methodological advance sprang. The telemetry system was designed to allow for instantaneous estimates of the intensity of children's activity and to allow for analysis of regular time-related changes or biorhythms in children's activity. It allowed this admirably, and the application of extant methods of time-series analysis to the data was successful. Then came the need to test hypotheses about effects of environmental manipulations on their biorhythms. Bohrer (1970) constructed and reported a new statistical test that allowed variance analysis techniques to be applied to spectral analysis. This method was used to test hypotheses concerning normal and retarded children, and can be counted as an advance.

Another success was the effort to build a procedure for the micro-analysis of a playful episode. It was obvious that the camera and telemetry system produced gross quantitive estimates of behavior. The telemetry system indicated the intensity of the child's activity. The camera system produced many measures of quantity (distance moved) and intensity (velocity of movement) and went a small way towards describing what the children were actually doing (group play in the open space). However, after many studies of gross activity it became obvious that play was a cognitive activity and that inferences about cognitions would require the analysis of the behaviors emitted in their serivce. Thus the analysis of behaviors had to move at the same speed as thinking. Aggregating behaviors over longer periods of time than a second or two would miss the dynamic interplay between the child's thinking and the child's overt behaviors.

Several attempts to undertake a fine-grain analysis were mounted but the one developed and reported by Barnett (1974) was the only one that produced any useful results, and they are reported in Chapter 5 and Appendix AVIII. All the micro-analyses shared one common feature; they required inferences concerning the intent of the child in emitting a response.

Much of the early thinking on defining play was that a behavior was play when it was playful. Playfulness was determined by the intent of the player. Thus the same response can, on different occasions, be work or play. Ellis (1973) uses this form of definition when arguing that play can be defined by motive. This observational method finally grasped this thorny issue and attempted to sort out individual responses according to their perceived intent. It was first used by Karlsson (1972) who broke down the behavior of hyperactive and normal children into episodes according to the perception of a unified theme to the behavior. This was the first use of an observer's capacity to perceive intention. Karlsson's work merely counted episodes but Barnett built on this and categorized behavior by the perceived intention.

While this may grate on some scientists' ears, it should not do so. Firstly, the taxonomy of the possible categories were written down beforehand. Secondly, it exploited a set of observational skills very well developed in adult humans. We all are much practiced in making inferences concerning the nature of the organizing intent behind others' streams of behaviors. We are continually making inferences from behaviors concerning intent because this allows higher fidelity predictions concerning what behavior comes next. It is not a magical or intuitive process. It is based on the data of myriad life experiences.

If one observer were to infer the intent of a response or stream of responses, could two observers agree? Theoretically the answer should be yes, providing they have been reared in a similar culture where the compound of messages and behaviors were similar. Two observers tested Barnett's system of categorizing the behaviors of children by intent. They were asked to categorize behaviors and record the times at which the intent of the activity changes. The two time-lines produced a correlation coefficient of $+.99$.

A most important tool available to researchers on play, the highly developed capacity of adults from the same culture to make reliable inferences as to the intention of another's behavior, has been ignored. Probably this has been so because it appeared unscientific to build science on an observer's inferences concerning intent. This reluctance was probably amplified by the aggressively publicized tenet of Watsonian behaviorism that behavioral science must restrict itself to the study of the directly observable and purge itself of intervening variables and hypothetical constructs like "intention." However, the processes whereby the observers can produce such reliable estimates will be analyzed and shown to be constructed from elements that can be described objectively. The decision to go ahead and start the research was based on the assumption that somehow adult observers could agree on the intent of a child's behavior. Although the steps followed by each were not clearly understood, it was decided to do the research and leave the analysis of the reasons for such close agreement till later.

Preview

This brings the theme followed by the research on activity and play to a fork in the path. On the one hand, play is like quicksilver, proceeding at the pace of thought. It needs to be studied at the same rate. On the other hand, important questions concerning the activity of children will be answered only by very long term studies encompassing more than one day. These long term studies are costly, and the prognosis for their being done in the immediate future is poor. However, until they are done such notions as normal activity, hyperactivity, and surplus energy, will not be illuminated.

Most of the research reported here was largely of the middle range running from studies of 4 to about 90 minutes. We await the sharpened vision of those who, with hindsight, can avoid the middle ranges and concentrate their energies on fine-grain analysis of acts or the long term analysis of days.

The work presented in this monograph was given shape by the view that children, when not preempted by external consequences, are rewarded by the processing of information and the arousal that is presumed to result. Children learn to emit responses that maximize the probability that appropriate information is generated.

Information or arousal seeking is but one source of behavior in a complex of sources. It is recognized that there can be no unifactored explanation for all behavior. Arousal or information seeking is but one source of incitement to action. But, it has been largely ignored by behavior science, despite the assertions made here that it is an important, perhaps crucial, source of influence.

The evidence presented here clearly scotches the notion that quiescence is the natural state of human organism. Children who were allowed to do what they wanted in a varied array of settings never stopped being active, apart from very short rests after strenuous bouts of activity necessitated by homeostatic pressures. Efforts were made by a variety of researchers to purge the setting of 'demand' for given behaviors, yet behavior consistently emerged. The conclusion is simple and straightforward. The well spring for this activity must lie within each individual child; the behavior is intrinsically motivated.

Our beliefs concerning the nature of this internal pressure to behave have been identified *ad nauseam* already. However, the kinds of behavior emitted are sensitive to the environment. The child uses the setting as a source of information. Time and again studies show that the environment strongly influences the behavior of the child. Children interact with the most appropriate source of information available. Wuellner showed that preference for old items could be destroyed by the addition of a novel but similar climbing apparatus, yet Lovelace showed that a bizarre object was approached more slowly than a familiar one. Scholtz showed that in simpler settings children began to traffic with their complex peers earlier than in complex settings rich in information. Gramza demonstrated how aversive a setting was that contained only a child and his or her clothing, and Barnett showed that once simple tasks were completed the children went on to interact with the apparatus and other items in the setting. Always, when free to do so, the children avoided quiescence but ingeniously probed the setting for further opportunities. They explored, investigated, and manipulated it increasingly, and if the experimenters successfully eliminated such opportunities the child used his or her own body.

There are common elements in this behavior that can usefully be described as information-seeking behavior. The individual, along with the cognitive nature of the definition of what information is, fits well with the long standing notions that what is playful is internally determined. The notion suggests how to interpret the data and how to manage the setting to allow for playful behavior. In our opinion, the concept that information seeking is a complex of behaviors maintained by the presumed rewards of consuming information should be accepted. We are not so sure that we can recommend the acceptance of the additional elements in the model that postulated that the intervening mechanisms are rooted in the biology of arousal. It makes sense that they should. The information-seeking model requires the interposition of a comparator (Does this stimulus resolve an uncertainty?) and a signalling mechanism that triggers a rewarding sensation (when it does). The proposed arousal-seeking model, using the patchy knowledge of arousal and filling in the gaps, cheerfully added the presumed intervening mechanisms. Unfortunately, the associated arousal level changes have not yet been clearly demonstrated.

Those who are happy to invade the black-box can continue to search for what goes on inside. Those who are happy to deal with behavior in terms of streams of antecedent and subsequent events and their statistical association can do so quite happily using the information-seeking notion without the necessity of introducing concepts like arousal.

Accepting the notion of information-seeking allows increased understanding of the hyperactive child. The findings concerning hyperactive children are consistent with the view that these children are not different in their needs for energy expenditure as their diagnostic categorization suggests. Two findings are significant. First, hyperactive children are indistinguishable from normal children in a free play setting. Second, the administration of the most popular drug for controlling hyperactivity in constrained settings (methylphenidate) produces no distinguishable effects on hyperactive children at play. Normal children are relatively quiescent in constrained settings and active in free play settings. Hyperactive children, however, are active in both. The conclusion to be reached here is that hyperactives are children with either a relatively great need for information or who cannot inhibit their probing for information in settings where such behavior is forbidden. Hyperactive children seem to exemplify a high level of playfulness that is successfully diminished in constrained settings by medication. The desire to inhibit this high level playfulness, on the part of others, overlays the child's hyperactivity with all kinds of social constraints which, it is suspected, disturbs other aspects of their behavior. It is clear though that hyperactivity is a social problem that stems from the inability of the child to inhibit undesired information generating behavior. The problem falls away when the constraints are relaxed. From an evolutionary viewpoint it is claimed that a high level propensity for exploratory and manipulatory behaviors is beneficial. Hyperactive children may well represent the super-normal in the spectrum of behavioral variability.

Other evidence suggests this to be the case. Wade in his study of profound-ly retarded children found that their behavior was of low intensity, diffuse, and random. Although the children were labeled hyperactive in their institution, their activity levels were shown to be relatively low and that they rarely interacted with the environment to produce effects. It was as if these children did not possess the wherewithal to extract information from the setting, and it was the featurelessness of their behavior that became obtrusive leading to their isolation from society and their being labeled hyperactive by an institution. The need for different labels for the activity of these two classes of children was identified clearly by Karlsson. The fea-tureless activity she called hyperkinetic, and in one sense these are unsuccess-ful humans who in more primitive settings would have been at an even greater selective disadvantage. Hyperactives, on the other hand, providing the social constraints visited on them do not damage them in other ways, may well be highly successful. The followup has not been done, but highly active people are highly prized in adult society, and it may well be that the very children who could not, or refused to, bow to constraint are prized in later life.

We have shown that peers are a powerful source of influence. Children in their search for information frequently turned to the actions of their peers. Social interaction was a powerful source of reinforcement. This is presumably the source of children's socialization. Our data showed that it was extremely difficult to design settings able to sustain solitary or non-interactive play, and the physical environment soon lost the competition for attention to interac-tions with peers. This finding bears a family resemblance to other literature, particularly primate socialization work, that shows peer interaction to be a powerful source of influence.

The work reported here for ethical reasons could not go to the heroic lengths possible in primate socialization studies. Our work here had to be content with making inferences from the results of pitting the physical versus the social setting in their effects on play. The formal evidence presented here is simple; there exists a preference for peer over object interaction. We argue that in the long run other children are far richer sources of information than even the most complex objects that we could build for the playroom.

Given that peers are usually preferred, it is possible to deal in general terms with the attributes of physical objects that make them more preferable.

Gramza, after his long series of preference studies, concluded that no one attribute, color, position, encapsulation, height, etc. would guarantee a capacity to capture and engage the attention of the children. In specific combinations, though, these elements may well provide the *functional complexity* necessary to generate a stream of exploratory, investigatory, and manipulatory responses that we have called play. Functional complexity is a term used to try to bring together the notions that attractive play objects are objects complex in what can be done with them. Information comes from the interactive possibilities rather than the complexity of the object itself. Objects that are responsive or support a stream of responses that can escalate in complexity are desirable. The most functionally complex objects are those that require the addition of another child. There the functional complexity and the responsive uncertainties are multiplied by the complexities of the playmate.

Good design for play environments must recognize the crucial role of peers in the immediate processes of play and that objects should be designed to maximize their functional complexity.

Toward the end of the period covered here we began to realize that nearly all the work done had concentrated on the analysis of the effect of manipulating stimuli from the environment. However, the information seeking model (Ellis, 1973) had referred to uncertainties inherent in the response. Clearly the probabilities that are inherent in mounting a response also contain information. In fact, learning involves attending to the disparity between what was intended and what took place. The information is at a maximum when the various response possibilities are equally probable. Thus the process of learning is of itself intrinsically rewarding. This explains the heavy "learning" content of most recreational programs and hobbies and is a rather severe criticism of the educational system that overcomes the intrinsically rewarding nature of learning for most people. The rewards inherent in uncertainty seem ill-understood by teachers. When the material is too difficult or too easy then the probability of making an appropriate response is not rewarding; random responding and repetition are work and have to be sustained by extrinsic rewards.

The model also specifically included the notion of epistemic behavior advanced by Berlyne. Thus cognitive activity or thinking could generate and resolve uncertainties. This activity has not led to easily detectable responses; in fact, we were unable to detect these at all, but must be seen as an intervening behavior.

Thus what has emerged is: information can be received merely from the environment, can be generated in the environment by the emission of responses producing effects containing information, or can be generated in nervous system of the individual by the combination of symbolic representations of experience and extrapolations from that experience.

Future analyses of play behavior must recognize the interactive role of events in the environment caused by other phenomena or the players themselves, plus the critical central ingredient, the higher processes accompanying those events. Thus, the legitimate study of play must include the study of the topography of the stimulus field, the topography of the response, together with the cognitive activity of the player. To deal with only one set of phenomena begs the essential complexity of human play behavior.

Bibliography

1. Allen, A. H. B. *Pleasure and Instinct.* New York: Harcourt, Brace & Co., 1930.

2. Amen, E. W., and N. Ranson. "A Study of the Relationship between Play Patterns and Anxiety in Young Children." *Genetic Psychology Monographs,* 50 (1954), 5–41.

3. Argyris, C. "Some Unintended Consequences of Rigorous Research." *Psychological Bulletin,* 70 (1968), 185–97.

4. Arkes, H. R., and A. W. Boykin. "Analysis of Complexity Preference in Head Start and Nursery School Children." *Perceptual and Motor Skills,* 33 (1971), 1131–37.

5. Aronfreed, J. "Imitation and Identification: An Analysis of Some Affective and Cognitive Mechanisms." Paper presented at the biennial meeting of the Society for Research in Child Development. New York, March 1967.

6. Aronfreed, J. "The Concept of Internalization." In *Handbook of Socialization Theory and Research,* edited by D. A. Goslin. Chicago: Rand McNally, 1969.

7. Atkinson, B. R. "The Effect of Activity and Social Stimulation on Attention." Unpublished PhD dissertation, University of Western Ontario, 1970.

8. Azrin, N. H., and O. R. Lindsley. "The Reinforcement of Cooperation between Children." *Journal of Abnormal and Social Psychology,* 52 (1956), 100–102.

9. Bain, A. *The Senses and the Intellect (3rd. Ed.).* London: Longmans Green, 1868.

10. Baldwin, J. D. "The Ontogeny of Social Behavior of Squirrel Monkeys (Saimiri Sciureus) in a Semi-natural Environment." *Folia Primatol.,* 11 (1969), 35–79.

11. Baltes, P. M., L. R. Schmidt, and E. E. Boesch. "Preference for Different Visual Stimulus Sequences in Children, Adolescents and young Adults." *Psychonomic Science,* 11 (1968), 271–72.

12. Banks, M. D. "Interactive Effects of Conceptual Development of Parents and Teachers on Enhancing Creativity and Conditions on (sic) Home Play." Unpublished PhD dissertation, University of Illinois, 1973.

13. Barker, M. *A Technique for Studying the Social-Material Activities of Young Children.* New York: Columbia University Press (Child Development Monograph No. 3), 1930.

132

14. Barnett, L. A. "An Information Processing Model of Children's Play." Unpublished MS dissertation, University of Illinois, 1974; and a paper presented to the Second International Symposium on Play, Atlanta, Georgia, 1974.

15. Barnett, L. A., M. J. Ellis, and R. J. Korb. "Arousal Modulation as a Function of Visual Complexity." Abstract describing a project in progress. Annual Report of the MPPRL, Children's Research Center, University of Illinois, 1974.

16. Bartol, C. R., and N. L. Pielstick. "The Effects of Ambiguity, Familiarization, Age and Sex on Stimulus Preference." *Journal of Experimental Child Psychology*, 14 (1972), 21–9.

17. Beach, F. A. "Current Concepts of Play in Animals." *American Naturalist*, 79, (1945), 523–41.

18. Berlyne, D. E. "Novelty and Curiosity as Determinants of Exploratory Behavior." *British Journal of Psychology*, 41 (1950), 68–80.

19. Berlyne, D. E. "The Arousal and Satiation of Perceptual Curiosity in the Rat." *Journal of Comparative Physiological Psychology*, 48 (1955), 238–46.

20. Berlyne, D. E. *Conflict, Arousal and Curiosity*. New York: McGraw-Hill, 1960.

21. Berlyne, D. E. "Complexity and Incongruity Variables and Determinants of Exploratory Choice and Evaluative Ratings." *Canadian Journal of Psychology*, 17 (1963), 274–90. (a)

22. Berlyne, D. E. "Motivational Problems Raised by Exploratory and Epistemic Behavior." In *Psychology: A Study of Science*, Vol. 5, edited by S. Koch. New York: McGraw-Hill, 1963, 284–364. (b)

23. Berlyne, D. E. "Emotional Aspects of Learning." *Ann. Rev. Psychol.*, 15 (1964), 115–42.

24. Berlyne, D. E. *Structure and Direction of Thinking*. New York: Wiley, 1965.

25. Berlyne, D. E. "Curiosity and Exploration." *Science*, 153 (1966), 25–33.

26. Berlyne, D. E. "Arousal and Reinforcement." In *Nebraska Symposium on Motivation, 1967*, edited by D. Levine. Lincoln: University of Nebraska Press, 1967.

27. Berlyne, D. E. "Laughter, Humor and Play." In *The Handbook of Social Psychology*, Vol. 3. edited by G. Lindzey and E. Aronson. London: Addison-Wesley Publishing Co., 1969, 795–852.

28. Berlyne, D. E. "Novelty, Complexity, and Hedonic Value." *Perception & Psychophysics*, 8(5A) (1970), 279–86.

29. Berlyne, D. E. "Effects of Auditory Prechoice Stimulation on Visual Exploratory Choice." *Psychonomic Science*, 25 (1971), 193–94.

30. Berlyne, D. E., M. A. Craw, P. H. Salapatek, and J. L. Lewis. "Novelty, Complexity, Incongruity, Extrinsic Motivation and the GSR." *Journal of Experimental Psychology*, 66 (1963), 560–67.

31. Berlyne, D. E., and J. B. Crozier. "Effects of Complexity and Prechoice Stimulation on Exploratory Choice." *Perception & Psychophysics*, 10 (1971), 242–46.

32. Berlyne, D. E., and P. McDonnell. "Effect of Stimulus Complexity and Incongruity on Duration of EEG Desynchronization." In *Current Research in Motivation*, edited by R. N. Haber. New York: Holt, Rinehart & Winston, 1966, 306–11.

33. Biehler, R. F. "Companion Choice Behavior in the Kindergarten." *Child Development*, 25 (1954), 45–50.

34. Bishop, D. W., and C. A. Chace. "Parental Conceptual Systems, Home Play Environments and Potential Creativity in Children." *Journal of Experimental Child Psychology*, 12 (1971), 318–38.

35. Black, K. N., T. M. Williams, and D. R. Brown. "A Developmental Study of Preschool Children's Preference for Random Forms." *Child Development*, 42 (1971), 57–61.

36. Blurton-Jones, N. G., ed. *Ethological Studies of Child Behavior*. Cambridge, England: Cambridge University Press, 1972.

37. Bohrer, R. E. "A Modified Grenander-Rosenblatt Test." Unpublished paper, Department of Mathematics, University of Illinois, 1970.

38. Bradfield, R. B., P. B. Huntzicker, and G. J. Fruehan. "Simultaneous Comparison of Respirometer and Heart Rate Telemetry Techniques as Measures of Human Energy Expenditure." *American Journal of Clinical Nutrition*, 22 (1969), 696–700.

39. Brand, E. D., R. E. Stetson, J. R. Beall, T. L. Lennard, L. J. Epstein, and D. C. Ransom. Letters to the Editor of *Science*, 170 (1970), 928–30.

40. Brennan, W. M., E. W. Ames, and R. W. Moore. *Science*, 151 (1966), 354.

41. Brickman, P., J. Redfield, A. A. Harrison, and R. Crandall. "Drive and Predisposition as Factors in the Attitudinal Effects of Mere Exposure." *Journal of Experimental Social Psychology*, 8 (1972), 31–44.

42. Bronson, G. W. "The Fear of Novelty." *Psychological Bulletin*, 69 (1968), 350–58.

43. Brown, J. S. "Pleasure-Seeking Behavior and the Drive-ReductionHypothesis." In *Current Research in Motivation*, edited by R. N. Haber. New York: Holt, Rinehart & Winston, 1966.

44. Bruner, J. S. *Processes of Cognitive Growth in Infancy*. Worcester, Mass.: Clark University Press, 1968.

45. Buehler, C. "The Child and Its Activity with Practical Material." *British Journal of Educational Psychology*, 3 (1933), 27–41.

46. Buehler, C. "Motivation and Personality." *Dialectica*, 5 (1951), 312–61.

47. Buehler, C., H. Hetzer, and F. Mabel. "Die Affektwirksamkeit von Fremdheitseindruecken im ersten Lebensjahr." *Zeitschrift fuer Psychologie*, 107 (1928), 30–49.

48. Buehler, K. *Abriss der geistigen Entwicklung des Kindes*. Leipzig: Quelle & Meyer, 1919.

49. Buehler, K. "Displeasure and Pleasure in Relation to Activity." In *Feelings and Emotions: The Wittenberg Symposium*, edited by M. L. Reymert. Worcester, Mass.: Clark University Press, 1928.

50. Buehler, K. *The Mental Development of the Child*. New York: Harcourt, Brace & Company, 1930.

51. Burgess, T. D. G., and S. M. Sales. "Attitudinal Effects of Mere Exposure: A Reevaluation." *Journal of Experimental Social Psychology*, 7 (1971), 461–72.

52. Butler, R. A. "Discrimination Learning by Rhesus Monkeys to Visual Exploration Motivation." *Journal of Comparative and Physiological Psychology*, 46 (1953), 95–98.

53. Butler, R. A., and H. F. Harlow. "Persistence of Visual Exploration in Monkeys." *Journal of Comparative and Physiological Psychology*, 47 (1954), 258–63.

54. Butler, R. A. "The Differential Effect of Visual and Auditory Incentives on the Performance of Monkeys." *American Journal of Psychology*, 71 (1958), 591–93.

55. Cannon, W. B. *The Wisdom of the Body*. New York: Norton, 1932.

56. Cantor, G. N. "Responses of Infants and Children to Complex and Novel-Stimulation." In *Advances in Child Development and Behavior*, Vol. I, edited by L. P. Lipsitt and C. C. Spiker. New York: Academic Press, 1963.

57. Cantor, G. N. "Children's Like-Dislike Ratings of Familiarized and Non-familiarized Visual Stimuli." *Journal of Experimental Child Psychology*, 6 (1968), 651–57.

58. Cantor, G. N. "Effects of Stimulus Familiarization on Child Behavior." In *Minnesota Symposia on Child Psychology*, Vol. 3, edited by J. P. Hill. Minneapolis: University of Minnesota Press, 1969.

59. Cantor, G. N. "Effects of Familiarization on Children's Ratings of Pictures of Whites and Blacks." *Child Development*, 43 (1972), 1219–29.

60. Cantor, G. N., and S. K. Kubose. "Preschool Children's Ratings for Familiarized and Nonfamiliarized Visual Stimuli." *Journal of Experimental Child Psychology*, 8 (1969), 74–81.

61. Cantor, J. H., and G. N. Cantor. "Observing Behavior in Children as a Function of Stimulus Novelty." *Child Development*, 35 (1964), 119–28. (a)

62. Cantor, J. H., and G. N. Cantor. "Children's Observing Behavior as Related to Amount of Recency of Stimulus Familiarization. *Journal of Experimental Child Psychology*, 1 (1964), 241–47. (b)

63. Cantor, J. H., and G. N. Cantor. "Functions Relating Children's Observing Behavior to Amount and Recency of Stimulus Familiarization." *Journal of Experimental Psychology*, 72 (1966), 859–63.

64. Caron, R. F. "Visual Reinforcement of Head-Turning in Young Infants." *Journal of Experimental Child Psychology*, 5 (1967), 489–511.

65. Caron, R. F., and A. J. Caron. "Degree of Stimulus Complexity and Habituation of Visual Fixation in Infants. *Psychonomic Science*, 14 (1969), 78–79.

66. CIBA Pharmaceutical Company. Information sheet distributed with Ritalin, May, 1967.

67. Cockrell, D. L. "A Study of the Play of Children of Preschool Age by an Unobserved Observer." *Genetic Psychology Monographs*, 17 (1935), 379–469.

68. Cofer, C. N., and M. H. Appley. *Motivation: Theory and Research*. New York: Wiley, 1964.

69. Conners, C. K. "A Teacher Rating Scale for Use in Drug Studies with Children." *American Journal of Psychiatry*, 126 (1969), 152–56.

70. Consolazio, C. F., R. E. Johnson, and L. J. Pecora. *Physiological Measurements of Metabolic Functions in Man*. New York: McGraw-Hill, 1963.

71. Cottrell, N. B. "Social Facilitation in Cockroaches (1)." In *Social Facilitation and Imitative Behavior*, edited by E. Simmel, R. Hoppe, and G. Milton. Boston: Allyn & Bacon, 1968.

72. Cottrell, N. B. "Social Facilitation." In *Experimental Social Psychology*, edited by C. G. McClintock. New York: Holt, Rinehart & Winston, 1972.

73. Craig, T. T. "Analysis of Movement Patterns Using the Fish-Eye Camera and Coordinate System: The Reliability and Accuracy of the System Using Differ-

ent Sample Intervals." Internal report. Motor Performance & Play Research Laboratory, Children's Research Center, University of Illinois, 1969.

74. Cramer, E. M., and R. D. Bock. "Multivariate Analysis." *Review of Educational Research*, 36 (1966), 604–17.

75. Crook, W. G. "An alternate method of managing the hyperactive child." Letter to the editor of *Pediatrics*, November, 1974, 656.

76. Cushing, A. M. "A Perseverative Tendency in Preschool Children." *Arch. Psychol.*, 17 (1929), No. 108.

77. Davenport, R. K., and E. W., Menzel, Jr., "Stereotyped Behavior of the Infant Chimpanzee." *Archives of General Psychiatry*, 8, (1963), 99–104.

78. Dember, W. N. "Alternation Behavior." In *Functions of Varied Experience*, edited by D. W. Fiske and S. R. Maddi. Homewood, Illinois: Dorsey Press, 1961.

79. Dember, W. N., and R. W. Earl. "Analysis of Exploratory, Manipulatory, and Curiosity Behaviors." *Psychological Review*, 64 (1957), 91–96.

80. Dent, O. B., and E. C. Simmel. "Preference for Complex Stimuli as an Index of Diversive Exploration." *Perceptual and Motor Skills*, 26 (1968), 896–98.

81. Dewey, J. "Play." In *A Cyclopedia of Education*, edited by Paul Monore. New York: Macmillan Co., 1925.

82. DHEW. "Report of the Conference on the Use of Stimulant Drugs in the Treatment of Behaviorally Disturbed Young School Children." Office of Child Development, Washington, D.C.: Government Printing Office, 1971.

83. Dickerson, A. E. "The Relation of Play to Mental Development in Infancy and Preschool Years." Unpublished course work, University of Illinois, 1973.

84. Dow, M. "Playground Behavior Differentiating Artistic from Non-artistic Children." *Psychological Monographs*, 45 (1933), 82–94.

85. Duncker, K. "On Pleasure, Emotion, and Striving." *Philosophy and Phenomenological Research*, 1 (1940/41), 391–430.

86. Eliot, H. R., and S. E. Blow. *The Mottoes and Commentaries of Friedrich Froebel's "Mother Play"*. New York: Appleton & Co., 1909.

87. Ellis, M. J. "Sensorirhesis as a Motive for Play and Stereotyped Behavior." Internal report. Motor Performance & Play Research Laboratory, Children's Research Center, University of Illinois, 1969.

88. Ellis, M. J. "The Rational Design of Playgrounds." *Education Product Information Exchange Report*, 3 (1970), 3–6.

89. Ellis, M. J. "Play and Its Theories Re-examined." *Parks and Recreation*, August, (1971), 51–55.

90. Ellis, M. J. "Play: Theory and Research." In *Environmental Design*, edited by W. J. Mitchell. Proceedings of the EDRA 3/AR 8 conference, University of California at Los Angeles, January, 1972. (a)

91. Ellis, M. J. "Play: Practice and Research in the 1970s. Part 1: Why Do Children Play." *Journal for Health, Physical Education, and Recreation: Leisure Today*, June (1972), 29–31. (b)

92. Ellis, M. J. "Play, Creativity and Leadership." An interpretive paper. Presented to the 5th Congress of the International Playground Association, Vienna, September 1972. (c)

93. Ellis, M. J. *Why People Play*. Englewood Cliffs, N. J.: Prentice-Hall, 1973.

94. Ellis, M. J., L. A. Barnett, and R. J. Korb. "Psycho-physiological Correlates

of Play." Abstract describing an uncompleted project. Annual Report of the MPPRL, Children's Research Center, University of Illinois, 1973.

95. Ellis, M. J., and T. T. Craig. "A Note on the Inferiority of Retardates' Motor Performance." *Journal of Motor Behavior,* 1 (1969), 341–46.

96. Ellis, M. J., M. G. Wade, and R. E. Bohrer. "Short Biorhythms in Children's Play." Unpublished Technical Report. Motor Performance & Play Research Laboratory, Children's Research Center, University of Illinois, 1970.

97. Ellis, M. J., P. A. Witt, R. Reynolds, and R. C. Sprague. "Methylphenidate and the Activity of Hyperactives in the Informal Setting." *Child Development,* 45 (1974), 217–20.

98. Ellis, N. R., and R. S. Pryor. "Quantification of Gross Bodily Activity in Children with Severe Neuro-pathology." *American Journal of Mental Deficiency,* 63 (1959), 1034–37.

99. Endsley, R. C. "Effects of Differential Prior Exposure on Preschool Children's Subsequent Choice of Novel Stimuli." *Psychonomic Science,* 7 (1967), 411–12.

100. Faw, T. T., and J. C. Nunnally. "The Influence of Stimulus Complexity, Novelty, and Affective Value on Children's Visual Fixations." *Journal of Experimental Child Psychology,* 6 (1968), 141–53.

101. Fiske, D. W., and S. R. Maddi, (eds.). *Functions of Varied Experience.* Homewood, Illinois: Dorsey Press, 1961.

102. Forest, I. *Preschool Education.* New York: Macmillan, 1927.

103. Foster, L. E. "Determination of the Reliability and Validity of the Portable Respiratory Helmet." Unpublished internal report. Motor Performance & Play Research Laboratory, Children's Research Center, University of Illinois, 1971.

104. Fowler, H. *Curiosity and Exploratory Behavior.* New York: Macmillan, 1965.

105. Fowler, H. "Satiation and Curiosity: Constructs for a Drive and Incentive-motivation Theory of Exploration." In *The Psychology of Learning and Motivation: Advances in Research and Theory.* Vol. 1, edited by K. W. Spence and J. T. Spence. New York: Academic Press, 1967.

106. Frazier, T. W. Personal communication. Walter Reed Research Institute. Washington D.C., 1970.

107. Freud, S. *Beyond the Pleasure Principle.* New York: Bantam Books, 1970.

108. Froebel, F. W. A. *Die Menschenerziehung, die Erziehungs-Unterrichts und Lehrkunst, angestrebt in der allgemeinen deutschen Erziehungsanstalt zu Keilhau, dargestellt von dem Vorsteher derselben. 1. Band bis zum begonnenen Knabenalter.* Keilhau, 1826. Verlag der Anstalt. Leipzig in Commission bei C. F. Doerffling, 497S.

109. Froebel, F. W. A. *The Education of Man,* transl. by W. T. Harris. New York: Appleton, 1887.

110. Froebel, F. W. A. *The Education of Man,* transl. by W. N. Hailman. New York: Appleton, 1896.

111. Geeseman, R., and M. G. Wade. "A Heartrate Telemetry System to Study Activity of Children During Free Play." *Research Quarterly,* 42 (1971), 450–53.

112. Gilmore, J. B. "The Role of Anxiety and Cognitive Factors in Children's Play Behavior." *Child Development,* 37 (1966), 397–416. (a)

113. Gilmore, J. B. "Play: A Special Behavior." In *Current Research in Motivation,* edited by R. N. Haber. New York: Holt, Rinehart & Winston, 1966. (b)

114. Glanzer, M. "Changes and Interrelations in Exploratory Behavior." *Journal of Comparative and Physiological Psychology*, 54 (1961), 433–38.

115. Gramza, A. F. "Preferences of Preschool Children for Enterable Play Boxes." *Perceptual and Motor Skills*, 31 (1970), 177–78.

116. Gramza, A. F. "New Directions for the Design of Play Environments." Paper presented at the National Symposium on Park, Recreation and Environmental Design. Chicago, February 16, 1971.

117. Gramza, A. F. "Stimulus Factors Affecting Children's Use of Enterable Play Boxes." Internal report. Motor Performance & Play Research Laboratory, Children's Research Center, University of Illinois, 1972. (a)

118. Gramza, A. F. "A Measured Approach to Improvement of Play Environments." *Journal of Health, Physical Education, and Recreation: Leisure Today*, (1972) 43. (b)

119. Gramza, A. F. "An Analysis of Stimulus Dimensions which Define Children's Encapsulating Play Objects." Internal report. Motor Performance & Play Research Laboratory, Children's Research Center, University of Illinois, 1973. (a)

120. Gramza, A. F. "Children's Play and Stimulus Factors of the Physical Environment." Internal report. Motor Performance & Play Research Laboratory, Children's Research Center, University of Illinois, 1973. (b)

121. Gramza, A. F. "Measured Approach to Designing Play Environments." Internal report. Motor Performance & Play Research Laboratory, Children's Research Center, University of Illinois, 1973. (c)

122. Gramza, A. F. "Stereotypies of Normal Children in a Boredom Setting." In preparation. 1974.

123. Gramza, A. F. "Responses to Manipulability in a Play Object." Internal report. Motor Performance & Play Research Laboratory, Children's Research Center, University of Illinois, 1975.

124. Gramza, A. F., J. Corush, and M. J. Ellis. "Children's Play on Trestles Differing in Complexity: A Study of Play Equipment Design." *Journal of Leisure Research*, 4 (1972), 303–11.

125. Gramza, A. F., and R. P. Reynolds. "Effects of a Varied Stimulus Environment on Stereotypies in Normal Children." In preparation, 1974.

126. Gramza, A. F., and G. J. L. Scholtz. "Children's Responses to Visual Complexity in a Play Setting." *Psychological Reports*, 35 (1974), 895–99.

127. Gramza, A. F., and P. A. Witt. "Choices of Colored Blocks in the Play of Preschool Children." *Perceptual and Motor Skills*, 29 (1969), 783–87.

128. Gramza, A. F., P. A. Witt, A. G. Linford, and C. Jeanrenaud. "Responses of Mongoloid Children to Colored Block Presentation." *Perceptual and Motor Skills*, 29 (1969), 1008.

129. Greenacre, P. "Play in Relation to Creative Imagination." *Psychoanalytic Study of the Child*, 14 (1959), 61–80.

130. Grenander, U., and M. Rosenblatt. *Statistical Analysis of Stationary Time Series.* New York: Wiley & Sons, 1957.

131. Groos, K. *The Play of Animals.* New York: Appleton, 1898.

132. Gullickson, G. R. "A Note on Children's Selection of Novel Auditory Stimuli." *Journal of Experimental Child Psychology*, 4 (1966), 158–62.

133. GutsMuths, J. *Spiele zur Uebung und Erholung des Koerpers und Geistes fuer die Jugend, ihre Erzieher.* Schnepfenthal: Im Verlage der Buchhandlung der Erziehungsanstalt, 1802. Dritte Verbesserte Auflage.

134. Haber, R. N. (ed.) *Current Research in Motivation.* New York: Holt, Rinehart & Winston, 1966.

135. Haber, R. N. "Discrepancy from Adaptation as a Source of Affect." *Journal of Experimental Psychology*, 56 (1958), 370–75.

136. Haigis, E. "Das Spiel als Begegnung. Versuch einer materialen Spieldeutung." *Zeitschrift fuer Psychologie*, 150, (1941), 92–167.

137. Haith, M. M. "A Semi-automatic Procedure for Measuring Changes in Position." *Journal of Experimental Child Psychology*, 3 (1966), 289–95.

138. Harlow, H. F. "Learning and Satiation of Response in Intrinsically Motivated Complex Puzzle Performance by Monkeys." *Journal of Comparative and Physiological Psychology*, 43 (1950), 289–94.

139. Harlow, H. "Mice, Monkeys, Men and Motives." *Psychological Review*, 60 (1953), 23–32.

140. Harlow, H. F., M. K. Harlow, and D. R. Meyer. "Learning Motivated by the Manipulation Drive." *Journal of Experimental Psychology*, 40 (1950), 228–34.

141. Harlow, H. F., M. K. Harlow, and S. J. Suomi. "From Thought to Therapy: Lessons from the Primate Laboratory." *American Scientist*, 59, No. 5 (1971).

142. Harlow, H. F., and G. E. McClearn. "Object Discrimination Learned by Monkeys on the Basis of Manipulation Motives." *Journal of Comparative and Physiological Psychology*, 47 (1954), 73–76.

143. Harris, L. "The Effects of Relative Novelty on Children's Choice Behavior." *Journal of Experimental Child Psychology*, 2 (1965), 297–305.

144. Harrison, A. A. "Exposure, Favorability and Item Endorsement." *Psychological Reports*, 23 (1968), 1970. (a)

145. Harrison, A. A. "Response Competition, Frequency, Exploratory Behavior, and Liking." *Journal of Personality and Social Psychology*, 9 (1968), 363–68. (b)

146. Harrison, A. A. "Exposure and Popularity." *Journal of Personality*, 37 (1969), 359–77.

147. Harrison, A. A., and P. Hines, "The Effects of Frequency of Exposure at Three Short Exposure Times on Affective Ratings and Exploratory Behavior." Proceedings of the 78th annual convention of the American Psychological Association, 1970, 391–92.

148. Harrison, A. A., R. M. Tutone, and McFadgen, D. G. "Effects of Frequency of Exposure of Changing and Unchanging Stimulus Pairs on Affective Ratings." *Journal of Personality and Social Psychology*, 20, (1971), 102–11.

149. Harrison, A. A., and R. B. Zajonc. "The Effects of Frequency and Duration of Exposure on Response Competition and Affective Ratings." *Journal of Psychology*, 75 (1970), 163–70.

150. Harvey, O. J. "Cognitive Determinants of Role Playing." Tech. Contr. Report No. 1147 (07), University of Colorado, 1963.

151. Harvey, O. J. "System Structure, Flexibility and Creativity." In *Experience, Structure and Adaptability*, edited by O. J. Harvey. New York: Springer, 1966.

152. Harvey, O. J. Cited by but not referenced by Banks, M. D. "Interactive Effects

of Conceptual Development of Parents and Teachers on Enhancing Creativity and Condition of Home Play." Unpublished PhD dissertation. University of Illinois, 1973.

153. Hayes, J. R. "The Maintenance of Play in Young Children." *Journal of Comparative and Physiological Psychology*, 51 (1958), 788–94.

154. Hebb, D. O. "On the Nature of Fear." *Psychological Review*, 53 (1946), 259–76.

155. Hebb, D. O. *The Organization of Behavior*. New York: Wiley, 1949.

156. Hebb, D. O. "Drives and the CNS (Conceptual Nervous System)." *Psychological Review*, 62 (1955), 243–54.

157. Hebb, D. O. *A Textbook of Psychology*. Philadelphia: Saunders, 1966.

158. Hebb, D. O., and A. H. Riesen. "The Genesis of Irrational Fears." *Bulletin of the Canadian Psychological Association*, 3 (1943), 49–50.

159. Hebb, D. O., and W. R. Thompson. "The Social Significance of Animal Studies." In *Handbook of Social Psychology*, edited by G. Lindzey. Cambridge, Mass.: Addison-Wesley, 1954.

160. Helson, H. "Adaptation-level as Frame of Reference for Prediction of Psychophysical Data." *American Journal of Psychology*, 60, (1947), 1–29.

161. Helson, H. "Adaptation-level as a Basis for a Quantitative Theory of Frames of Reference." *Psychological Review*, 55 (1948), 297–313.

162. Helson, H. "Adaptation-level Theory." In *Psychology: A Study of Science*, Vol. I. edited by S. Koch. New York: McGraw-Hill, 1959.

163. Heron, W. "The Pathology of Boredom". *Scientific American*, January Vol. I 1957.

164. Herring, A., and H. L. Koch. "A Study of Some Factors Influencing the Interest-span of Preschool Children." *Journal of Genetic Psychology*, 38 (1930), 249–79.

165. Herron, R. E., and M. J. Frobish. "Computer Analysis and Display of Movement Patterns." *Journal of Experimental Child Psychology*, 8 (1969), 40–44.

166. Herron, R. E., and R. W. Ramsden. "Continuous Monitoring of Overt Human Body Movement by Radio Telemetry: A Brief Review." *Perceptual and Motor Skills*, 24 (1967), 1303.

167. Herron, R. E., and R. W. Ramsden. "A Telepedometer for the Remote Measurement of Human Locomotor Activity." *Psychophysiology*, 4 (1967), 112–15.

168. Herron, R. E., and B. Sutton-Smith. *Child's Play*. New York: John Wiley, 1971.

169. Herron, R. E., and J. Weir. "Dual-camera Cinematography for Studying Motion Transducer Output Characteristics." *Perceptual and Motor Skills*, 26 (1968), 461–62.

170. Hicks, R. A., and S. Dockstader. "Cultural Deprivation and Preschool Children's Preferences for Complex and Novel Stimuli." *Perceptual and Motor Skills*, 27 (1968), 1321–22.

171. Higgins, J. M. "Social Behavior of Four-year-old Children during Outdoor Play in Day Care Centres." *Dissertation Abstract*, 27 (1966), 993–94.

172. Hinde, R. A. *Biological Base of Human Social Behavior*. Johannesburg: McGraw-Hill, 1974.

173. Hollis, J. H. "The Effects of Social and Non-social Stimuli on the Behavior of Profoundly Retarded Children." *American Journal of Mental Deficiency*, 69 (1965), 772–89.

174. Homans, G. C. *The Human Group*. New York: Harcourt, 1950.

175. Howell, M. C., G. W. Rever, and M. L. Scholl with F. Trowbridge, and A. Rutledge. "Hyperactivity in Children: Types, Diagnosis, Drug Therapy, Approaches to Management." *Clinical Paediatrics*, 11 (1972), 30–32.

176. Hull, C. L. *Principles of Behavior*. New York: Appleton-Century-Crofts, 1943.

177. Hummel, T. J., and J. R. Sligo. "Empirical Comparison of Univariate and Multivariate Analysis of Varience Procedures." *Psychological Bulletin*, 76 (1971), 49–57.

178. Hunt, J. McV. "Experience and the Development of Motivation: Some Reinterpretations." *Child Development*, 31 (1960), 489–504.

179. Hunt, J. McV. *Intelligence and Experience*. New York: Ronald, 1961.

180. Hunt, J. McV. "The Psychological Basis for Using Pre-school Enrichment as an Antidote for Cultural Deprivation." *Merrill-Palmer Quarterly*, 10 (1964), 209–48.

181. Hunt, J. McV. "Intrinsic Motivation and Its Role in Psychological Development." In *Nebraska Symposium on Motivation*, Vol. 13. edited by D. Levine. Lincoln, Nebraska: University of Nebraska Press, 1965.

182. Hunt, J. McV. "Toward a Theory of Guided Learning in Development." In *Giving Emphasis to Guided Learning*, edited by R. H. Ojemann and K. Pritchett. Clevelend, Ohio: Education Research Council, 1966.

183. Hunt, J. McV. "Evolution of Current Concepts of Intelligence and Intellectual Development." *American Montessori Society Bulletin*, 6 (1967), No. 4.

184. Hunt, J. McV. *The Challenge of Incompetence and Poverty*. Urbana, Illinois: University of Illinois Press, 1969.

185. Hurlock, E. B. "Experimental Investigations of Childhood Play." *Psychological Bulletin*, 31 (1934), 47–66.

186. Hutt, C. "Exploration and Play in Children." *Symposium of the Zoological Society of London*, 18 (1966), 61–81.

187. Hutt, C. "Exploration and Play in Children." In *Child's Play*, edited by R. E. Herron and B. Sutton-Smith. New York: Wiley & Sons, 1971.

188. Hutt, C. "Predictions from Play." *Nature*, 237 (1972), 171–72.

189. Hutt, C., and S. J. Hutt. "Effects of Environmental Complexity and Stereotyped Behavior of Children." *Animal Behavior*, 13 (1965), 1–4.

190. Hutt, C., S. J. Hutt, and C. Ounsted. "A Method for the Study of Children's Behavior." *Developmental Medicine and Child Neurology*, 5 (1963), 233–45.

191. Hutt, S. J., and C. Hutt. *Direct Observation and Measurement of Behavior*. Springfield, Illinois: Charles C. Thomas, 1970.

192. Jeanrenaud, C. Y. "Play Behavior of Young Children in a Novel Situation." Unpublished Master's thesis. University of Illinois, 1969.

193. Jeanrenaud, C. Y. "Novelty and Complexity as a Function of Preference for Visual Stimuli." Unpublished PhD dissertation. University of Illinois, 1971.

194. Jeanrenaud, C. Y., and A. G. Linford. "Effects of Perceived Novelty on Approach-Avoidance Behavior of Young Children." *Perceptual and Motor Skills*, 29 (1969), 491–94.

195. Johnson, G. E. *Education by Plays and Games*. New York: Ginn and Company, 1907.

196. Johnson, M. W. "The Effect on Behavior of Variations in the Amount of Play Equipment." *Child Development*, 6 (1935), 56–68.

197. Johnson, R. E., R. F. Robbins, R. Schilke, P. Mole, J. Harris, and D. Wakat. "A Versatile System for Measuring Oxygen Consumption in Man." *Journal of Applied Physiology*, 22 (1967), 377–79.

198. Jones, A. "Stimulus-Seeking Behavior." In *Sensory Deprivation: Fifteen Years of Research*, edited by J. P. Zubek. New York: Appleton-Century-Crofts, 1969.

199. Jones, A., and D. W. McGill. "The Homeostatic Character of Information Drive in Humans." *Journal of Experimental Research in Personality*, 2 (1967), 25–31.

200. Kagan, J. "Attention and Psychological Change in the Child." *Science*, 170 (1970), 826–32.

201. Kagan, J. "Motives and Development." *Journal of Personality and Social Psychology*, 22 (1972), 51–66.

202. Karlsson, K. A. "Height Preferences of Children at Play." Unpublished Master's Thesis. University of Illinois, 1969.

203. Karlsson, K. A. "Comparison of Data Collection Systems." Internal report. Motor Performance & Play Research Laboratory, Children's Research Center, University of Illinois, 1970.

204. Karlsson, K. A. "Research on Children's Play, an Interpretive Paper." Internal report. Motor Performance & Play Research Laboratory, Children's Research Center, University of Illinois, 1971.

205. Karlsson, K. A. "Hyperactivity and Environmental Compliance." Unpublished PhD dissertation. University of Illinois, 1971.

206. Karlsson, K. A., and M. J. Ellis. "Height Preferences of Young Children at Play." *Journal of Leisure Research*, 4 (1972), 33–42.

207. Kaufman, M. E., and H. Levitt. "A Study of Three Stereotyped Behaviors in Institutionalized Mental Defectives." *American Journal of Mental Deficiency*, 69 (1965), 467–73.

208. Kleitman, N. *Sleep and Wakefulness*. Chicago: University of Chicago Press, 1963.

209. Klinger, E. "Development of Imaginative Behavior: Implications of Play for a Theory of Fantasy." *Psychological Bulletin*, 72 (1969), 277–98.

210. Korb, R. J. Personal communication, 1968.

211. Korb, R. J. Personal communication, 1972.

212. Korb, R. J. "A Simple Electrogoniometer: A Technical Note." *Research Quarterly*, 41(2) (1970), 203–5.

213. Kubose, S. K. "Motivational Effects of Boredom on Children's Response Speeds." *Developmental Psychology*, 6(2), (1972), 302–5.

214. Landers, D. M. "Factors Relating to the Expression of Power in Children's Play Groups." Internal report. Motor Performance & Play Research Laboratory, Children's Research Center, University of Illinois, 1970.

215. Lauer, M. Personal communication, 1967.

216. Laufer, M., and E. Denhoff, "Hyperkinetic Behavior Syndromes in Children." *Journal of Pediatrics*, 50 (1957), 463–73.

217. Lazarus, M. *Ueber die Reize des Spiels*. Berlin: Duemmler, 1883.

218. Leckhart, B., *et al.* "Looking Time, Stimulus Complexity, and the Perceptual Deprivation Effect." *Psychonomic Science*, 26(2) (1972), 107–8.

219. Lehman, H. C., and P. A. Witty. *The Psychology of Play Activities.* New York: A. S. Barnes and Company, 1927.

220. Lennard, H. L., L. J. Epstein, A. Bernstein, and D. C. Ranson. "Hazards Implicit in Prescribing Psychoactive Drugs." *Science,* 169 (1970), 438–41.

221. Leuba, C. "Toward Some Integration of Learning Theories: The Concept of Optimal Stimulation." *Psychological Reports,* 1 (1955), 27–33.

222. Leuba, C. J. *Man: A General Psychology.* New York: Holt, Rinehart and Winston, 1961.

223. Levere, T. E., R. T. Bartus, G. W. Motlock, and F. D. Hart. "Arousal from Sleep: Responsiveness to Different Auditory Frequencies Equated for Loudness." *Physiology and Behavior,* Vol. 10 (1975), 53–7.

224. Levitt, H., and M. E. Kaufman. "Sound Induced Drive and Stereotyped Behavior in Mental Defectives." *American Journal of Mental Deficiency,* 69 (1965), 729–34.

225. Lieberman, J. N. "Playfulness and Divergent Thinking: An Investigation of Their Relationship at the Kindergarten Level." *Journal of Genetic Psychology,* 107 (1965), 219–24.

226. Lieberman, J. N. "Playfulness: An Attempt to Conceptualize a Quality of Play and of the Player." Paper presented at the meetings of the Eastern Psychological Association. New York, April, 1966.

227. Lindsley, D. B. "Studying Neuropsychology and Bodily Functions." In *Methods of Psychology,* edited by T. G. Andrews. New York: John Wiley & Sons, 1948.

228. Lindsley, D. B. "Psychophysiology and Motivation." In *Nebraska Symposium on Motivation, 1957,* edited by M. J. Jones. Lincoln: University of Nebraska Press, 1957.

229. Linford, A. G., and C. Y. Jeanrenaud. "A Behavioral Model for a Four Stage Theory of Play. In *Contemporary Sports Psychology,* edited by G. Kenyon. Chicago: The Athletic Institute, 1970.

230. Linford, A. G., and J. H. Duthie. "The Use of Operant Technology to Induce Sustained Exertion in Young, Trainable Down's Syndrome Children." In *Contemporary Sports Psychology,* edited by G. Kenyon. Chicago: The Athletic Institute, 1970.

231. Linford, A. G., C. Y. Jeanrenaud, K. A. Karlsson, P. Witt, and M. D. Linford. "A Computerized Analysis of Characteristics of Down's Syndrome and Normal Children's Free Play Patterns." *Journal of Leisure Research,* 3(1) (1971), 44–52.

232. Liss, E. "Play Techniques in Child Analysis." *American Journal of Orthopsychiatry,* 6 (1936), 17–22.

233. Lore, R. K. "Activity-drive Hypothesis: Effects of Activity Restriction." *Psychological Bulletin,* 70 (1968), 566–74.

234. Lott, A. J., and B. E. Lott. "Group Cohesiveness as Interpersonal Attraction: A Review of Relationships with Antecedent and Consequent Variables." *Psychological Bulletin,* 64(4) (1965), 259–309.

235. Lovelace, G. "Responses of Educable Mentally Handicapped and Normal Children to a Unique Plaything." Unpublished Master's thesis. University of Illinois, 1971.

236. Mackworth, J. *Vigilance and Attention.* Baltimore, Md.: Penguin, 1970.

237. Maddi, S. R. "Exploratory Behavior and Variation Seeking in Man." In

Functions of Varied Experience, edited by D. W. Fiske and S. R. Maddi. Homewood, Illinois: Dorsey Press, 1961.

238. Maddi, S. R. "Meaning, Novelty, and Affect: Comments on Zajonc's Paper." *Journal of Personality and Social Psychology* (Monograph Supplement), 9 (2, Pt. 2) (1968), 28–29.

239. Magoun, H. W. *The Waking Brain*. Springfield, Illinois: Charles Thomas, 1958.

240. Malmo, R. B. "Anxiety and Behavioral Arousal." *Psychological Review*, 64, No. 5 (1957).

241. Malmo, R. B. "Activation: A Neuropsychological Dimension." *Psychological Review*, 66 (1959), 367–86.

242. Marshall, H. R., and B. R. McCandless. "A Study in Prediction of Social Behavior of Preschool Children." *Child Development*, 28 (1957), 149–59.

243. Martens, R. "Effect of an Audience on Learning and Performance of a Complex Motor Skill." *Journal of Personality and Social Psychology*, 12 (1969), 252–60.

244. Martens, R. "Anxiety and Motor Behavior: A Review." *Journal of Motor Behavior*, 3 (1971), 151–80.

245. Martens, R. "People Errors in People Experiments." *Quest*, 20 (1973), 16–20.

246. Martens, R. *Social Psychology and Physical Activity*. New York: Harper & Row, 1975.

247. Martens, R., and D. W. Kennedy. "Prediction of Social Behavior of Preschool Children while Playing in the Free Range." Internal report. Motor Performance & Play Research Laboratory, Children's Research Center, University of Illinois, 1969.

248. Martens, R., and D. M. Landers. "Coaction Effects on a Muscular Endurance Task." *Research Quarterly*, 40 (1969), 733–37. (a)

249. Martens, R., and D. M. Landers. "Effects of Anxiety, Competition and Failure on Performance of a Complex Motor Task." *Journal of Motor Behavior*, 1 (1969), 1–10. (b)

250. Martens, R., and D. M. Landers. "Evaluation Potential as a Determinant of Coaction Effects." *Journal of Experimental Social Psychology*, 8 (1972), 347–59.

251. Matlin, M. W. "Response Competition as a Mediating Factor in the Frequency-Affect Relationship." *Journal of Personality and Social Psychology*, 16 (1970), 536–52.

252. Matlin, M. W. "Response Competition, Recognition, and Affect." *Journal of Personality and Social Psychology*, 19 (1971), 295–300.

253. McCall, R. B., and J. Kagan. "Individual Differences in the Infant's Distribution of Attention to Stimulus Discrepancy." *Developmental Psychology*, 2 (1969), 90–98.

254. McClelland, D. C., J. W. Atkinson, R. A. Clark, and E. I. Lowell. "The Affective Arousal Model of Motivation." In *Current Research in Motivation*, edited by R. N. Haber. New York: Holt, Rinehart and Winston, 1966.

255. McClelland, D. C. and R. A. Clark. "Discrepancy Hypothesis." In *Current Research in Motivation*, edited by R. N. Haber. New York: Holt, Rinehart and Winston, 1966.

256. Mendel, G. "Choice of Play Objects as a Function of Their Degree of Novelty." Unpublished Doctoral Dissertation. University of Chicago, 1962.

257. Mendel, G. "Children's Preferences for Differing Degrees of Novelty." *Child Development*, 36 (1965), 453–65.

258. Millar, S. *The Psychology of Play*. Harmondsworth: Penguin-Books, 1968.

259. Montgomery, K. C., and M. Segall. "Discrimination Learning Based upon the Exploratory Drive." *Journal of Comparative and Physiological Psychology*, 48 (1955), 225–28.

260. Mowrer, O. H. *Learning Theory and Behavior*. New York: Wiley, 1960.

261. Munsinger, H., and W. Kessen. "Uncertainty, Structure and Preference." *Psychological Monographs: General and Applied*, 78 (1964), 1–24.

262. Munsinger, H., W. Kessen, and M. Kessen. "Age and Uncertainty: Developmental Variation in Preference for Variability." *Journal of Experimental Child Psychology*, 1 (1964), 1–15.

263. Munsinger, H., and M. W. Weir. "Infant's and Young Children's Preference for Complexity." *Journal of Experimental Child Psychology*, 5 (1967), 69–73.

264. Newcomb, T. M. "The Prediction of Interpersonal Attraction." *American Psychologist*, 11 (1956), 575–86.

265. Nissen, H. W. "A Study of Exploratory Behavior in the White Rat by Means of the Obstruction Method." *Journal of Genetic Psychology*, 37 (1930), 361–76.

266. Odom, R. D. "Effects of Auditory and Visual Stimulus Deprivation and Satiation on Children's Performance in an Operant Task." *Journal of Experimental Child Psychology*, 1 (1964), 16–25.

267. Odom, R. D. "Children's Preferences for Differing Degrees of Novelty." *Child Development*, 36 (1965), 453–65.

268. Olds, J. "Pleasure Centers in the Brain." *Scientific American*, October, 1956.

269. Parten, M. "Leadership among Preschool Children." *Journal of Abnormal and Social Psychology*, 27 (1933), 430–40.

270. Perlman, D., and S. Oskamp. "The Effects of Picture Content and Exposure Frequency on Evaluations of Negroes and Whites." *Journal of Experimental Social Psychology*, 7 (1971), 503–14.

271. Piaget, J. *Play, Dreams and Imitation in Childhood*. New York: Norton and Company, 1962.

272. Pielstick, N. L., and A. B. Woodruff. "Exploratory Behavior and Curiosity in Two Age and Ability Groups of Children." *Psychological Reports*, 14 (1964), 831–38.

273. Pillsbury, W. B. *Attention*. New York: Macmillan, 1908.

274. Porges, S. W., and D. C. Raskin. "Respiratory and Heart Rate Components of Attention." *Journal of Experimental Psychology*, 81 (1969), 497–503.

275. Pryor, K. W., R. Haag, and J. O'Reilly. "The Creative Porpoise: Training for Novel Behavior." *Journal of Experimental Analysis of Behavior*, 12 (1969), 653–61.

276. Pycraft, W. P. *The Infancy of Animals*. London: Hutchinson and Company, 1912.

277. Rainwater, C. *The Play Movement in the United States; A Study of Community Recreation*. Chicago: University of Chicago Press, 1922.

278. Ramsden, R. W. "The Design and Construction of an Inexpensive Miniaturized Telemetry System for the Analysis of Pedal Locomotion in Humans." Unpublished Master's Thesis. University of Illinois, 1967.

279. Reynolds, R. P. "The Operant Training of Creativity in Children." Unpublished PhD Dissertation. University of Illinois, 1973.

280. Reynolds, R. P., and M. J. Ellis. "The Operant Training of Creativity in Children." Mimeo, 1974.

281. Rheingold, H. L. "The Effect of Environmental Stimulation upon Social and Exploratory Behavior in the Human Infant." In *Determinants of Infant Behavior*, edited by B. M. Foss. Methuen, 1961.

282. Rheingold, H. L., W. C. Stanley, and J. A. Cooley. "Method for Studying Exploratory Behavior in Infants." *Science*, 136 (1962), 1054–55.

283. Ross, H. S., H. L. Rheingold, and C. O. Eckerman. "Approach and Exploration of a Novel Alternative by 12-month-old Infants." *Journal of Experimental Child Psychology*, 13 (1972), 85–93.

284. Runkel, P. J., and J. E. McGrath. *Research on Human Behavior. A Systematic Guide to Method.* New York: Holt, Rinehart and Winston, 1972.

285. Russell, E. M., and G. A. Pearce. "Exploration of Novel Objects by Marsupials." *Behavior*, 40 (3–4) (1971), 312–22.

286. Sackett, G. P. "Effects of Rearing Conditions upon the Behavior of Rhesus Monkeys (Macaca Mulatta)". *Child Development*, 36 (1965), 855–66.

287. Saegert, S. C., and J. N. Jellison. "Effects of Initial Level of Response Competition and Frequency of Exposure on Liking and Exploratory Behavior." *Journal of Personality and Social Psychology*, 16 (1970), 533–58.

288. Saegert, S., W. Swap, and R. B. Zajonc. "Exposure, Context, and Interpersonal Attraction." *Journal of Personality and Social Psychology*, 25 (1973), 234–42.

289. Sapora, A. V., and E. D. Mitchell. *The Theory of Play and Recreation.* New York: Ronald Press, 1961.

290. Schick, C., R. P. McGlynn, and D. Woolam. "Perception of Cartoon Humor as a Function of Familiarity and Anxiety Level." *Journal of Personality and Social Psychology*, 24 (1972), 22–25.

291. Schlosberg, H. The Concept of Play. *Psychological Review*, 54 (1947), 229–31.

292. Schneirla, T. "The Concepts of Development in Comparative Psychology." In *The Concept of Development*, edited by D. B. Harris. Minneapolis: University of Minn. Press, 1957.

293. Scholtz, G. J. L. "Environmental Novelty and Complexity as Determinants of Children's Play." Unpublished PhD Dissertation. University of Illinois, 1973.

294. Scholtz, G. J. L., and M. J. Ellis. "Repeated Exposure to Objects and Peers in a Play Setting." *Journal of Experimental Child Psychology*, 19 (1975), 448–55. (a)

295. Scholtz, G. J. L., and M. J. Ellis. "Novelty, Complexity and Play." Paper presented at the International Seminar on Play in Physical Education and Sport. Wingate Institute, Israel, April, 1975. (b)

296. Schulman, J. L., J. C. Kaspar, and F. M. Throne. *Brain Damage and Behavior.* Springfield, Illinois: C. C. Thomas, 1965.

297. Schultz, D. P. *Sensory Restriction: Effects on Behavior.* New York: Academic Press, 1965.

298. Sherif, M., and C. Sherif. *Groups in Harmony and Tension.* New York: Harper, 1953.

299. Sherif, M., B. J. White, and O. J. Harvey. "Status in Experimentally Produced Groups." *American Journal of Sociology*, 60 (1955), 370–79.

300. Sidowski, J. B. *Experimental Methods and Instrumentation in Psychology.* New York: McGraw Hill, 1966.

301. Siebold, J. R. "Children's Rating Responses as Related to Amount and Recency of Stimulus Familiarization and Stimulus Complexity." *Journal of Experimental Child Psychology,* 14 (1972), 257–64.

302. Singer, J. L. *The Child's World of Make-Believe: Experimental Studies of Imaginative Play.* New York: Academic Press, 1973.

303. Skinner, B. F. *The Behavior of Organisms: An Experimental Approach.* New York: Appleton-Century, 1938.

304. Skinner, B. F. *Contingencies of Reinforcement.* New York: Appleton-Century-Crofts, 1969.

305. Smock, D. D., and B. G. Holt. "Children's Reactions to Novelty: An Experimental Study of Curiosity Motivation." *Child Development,* 33 (1962), 631–42.

306. Solomon, E. L. "The Colored Block Play of Three-year-old Children." Unpublished Master's Thesis. University of Illinois, 1970.

307. Solomon, P. (ed.). *Sensory Deprivation.* Cambridge, Mass: Harvard University Press, 1961.

308. Spence, J. T., and K. W. Spence. "The Motivational Components of Manifest Anxiety: Drive and Drive Stimuli." In *Anxiety and Behavior,* edited by C. D. Spielberger. New York: Academic Press, 1966.

309. Sprague, R. L., K. R. Barnes, and J. S. Werry. "Methylphenidate and Thioridazine; Learning, Activity and Behavior in Emotionally Disturbed Boys." *American Journal of Orthopsychiatry,* 40 (1970), 615–28.

310. Sprague, R. L. and M. J. Ellis. "Measurement and Treatment of Hyperactivity in Children." Contract proposal solicited by NICHHD. Department of Health, Education and Welfare, Washington, D. C., 1970.

311. Sprague, R. L., and E. K. Sleator. "Effects of Psychopharmacological Agents on Learning Disabilities." *Pediatric Clinics of North America,* 20 (1973), 719–35.

312. Sprague, R. L., J. S. Werry, and K. V. Davis. "Psychotropic Drug-Effects on Learning and Activity Level of Children." Paper presented at Gatlinburg Conference on Research and Theory in Mental Retardation, 1969.

313. Stevenson, A. H., and D. B. Lynn. "Preference for High Variability in Young Children." *Psychonomic Science,* 23 (1971), 143–44.

314. Stewart, M. A., F. M. Pitts, A. G. Craig, and W. Dieruf. "The Hyperactive Child Syndrome." *American Journal of Orthopsychiatry,* 36 (1966), 861–67.

315. Strain, G. S. "Preference for Complexity in Children's Color Choices." *Perceptual and Motor Skills,* 27 (1968), 1030.

316. Suedfeld, P. "Changes in Intellectual Performance and the Susceptibility to Influence." In *Sensory Deprivation: Fifteen Years of Research,* edited by J. P. Zubek. New York: Appleton-Century-Crofts, 1969.

317. Suomi, S. J. and H. F. Harlow. "Monkeys at Play." *Natural History Magazine, Special Supplement,* December, 1971.

318. Sutton-Smith, B. "The Role of Play in Cognitive Development." *Young Children,* 22 (1967), 361–70.

319. Sutton-Smith, B. "Novel Responses to Toys." *Merrill-Palmer Quarterly,* 14 (1968), 159–60.

320. Sutton-Smith, B. "Children at Play." *Natural History Magazine (Special Supplement)*, December, 1971, 54–59.

321. Sutton-Smith, B. "Play: The Mediation of Novelty." Address to Scientific Congress, fuer die Spiele der XX Olympiade, Muenchen (Section K11), August 21, 1972.

322. Sutton-Smith, B. "Play as a Transformational Set." In *Leisure Today*, edited by B. Sutton-Smith. Second special supplement to *Journal of Health, Physical Education and Recreation*, Summer, 1973.

323. Swinton, R. S. "Analysis of Child Behavior by Intermittent Photography." *Child Development*, 5 (1934), 292–93.

324. Taylor, D. W. "Toward an Information Processing Theory of Motivation." In *Nebraska Symposium on Motivation*, edited by M. R. Jones. Lincoln, Nebraska: University of Nebraska Press, 1960.

325. Tinbergen, N. *The Study of Instinct*. Oxford: Oxford University Press, 1950.

326. Tinklepaugh, O. L. "Social Behavior of Animals." In *Comparative Psychology (rev. ed.)*, edited by F. A. Moss. New York: Prentice-Hall, 1942.

327. Tizard, J. *Community Services for the Mentally Handicapped*. Oxford: Oxford University Press, 1964.

328. Torrance, E. P. "Education and Creativity." In *Creativity: Progress and Potential*, edited by C. W. Taylor. New York: McGraw Hill, 1964.

329. Torrance, E. P. *Rewarding Creative Behavior*. Englewood Cliffs, N.J.: Prentice-Hall, 1965.

330. Torrance, E. P. *Torrance Test of Creative Thinking: Directions Manual and Scoring Guide; Figural Test Booklet A. Research Edition*. Princeton, N.J.: Personnel Press, 1966.

331. Unikel, I. P. and C. N. Harris. "Experience and Preference for Complexity in Children's Choices." *Perceptual and Motor Skills*, 31 (1970), 757–58.

332. Van Alstyne, D. Play Behavior and Choice of Play Materials of Preschool Children. Chicago: University of Chicago Press, 1932.

333. Vitz, P. C. "Preferences for Different Amounts of Complexity." *Behavioral Sciences*, 6 (1966), 105–14.

334. Wada, T. "An Experimental Study of Hunger in Its Relation to Activity." *Archives of Psychology*, 57 (1922), 1.

335. Wade, G. R. "A Study of Free-play Patterns of Elementary-School Age Children in Playground Equipment Areas." Unpublished Master's Thesis. Pennsylvania State University, 1968.

336. Wade, M. G. "Biorhythms in Children During Free Play." Unpublished PhD Dissertation. University of Illinois, 1971.

337. Wade, M. G. "Biorhythms and Activity Level of Institutionalized Mentally Retarded Persons Diagnosed Hyperactive." *American Journal of Mental Deficiency*, 78 (1973), 262–67.

338. Wade, M. G. and M. J. Ellis. "Measurement of Free Range Activity in Children as Modified by Social and Environmental Complexity." *The American Journal of Clinical Nutrition*, 24 (1971), 1457–60.

339. Wade, M. G., M. J. Ellis, and R. E. Bohrer. "Biorhythms in the Activity of Children during Free Play." *Journal of the Experimental Analysis of Behavior*, 20 (1973), 155–62.

340. Wade, M. G., R. E. Herron, P. Schmitz, and G. A. Franklin, Jr. "Evaluation of a New Respirometer System Incorporating a NASA-designed Helmet." Internal report. Motor Performance & Play Research Laboratory, Children's Research Center, University of Illinois, 1971.

341. Walker, S. "Drugging the American Child: We're too Cavalier about Hyperactivity." *Psychology Today*, December 1974, 43–48.

342. Webb, E. J., A. T. Campbell, R. D. Schwartz, and L. Sechrest. *Unobtrusive Measures: Nonreactive Research in the Social Sciences.* Chicago: Rand McNally & Co., 1966.

343. Weizman, F., L. B. Cohen, and R. J. Pratt. "Novelty, Familiarity and the Development of Infant Attention." *Developmental Psychology*, 4 (1971), 149–54.

344. Welker, W. I. "Some Determinants of Play and Exploration in Chimpanzees." *Journal of Comparative and Physiological Psychology*, 49 (1956), 84–89. (a)

345. Welker, W. I. "Variability of Play and Exploratory Behavior in Chimpanzees." *Journal of Comparative and Physiological Psychology*, 49 (1956), 181–85. (b)

346. Welker, W. I. "Effects of Age and Experience on Play and Exploration of Young Chimpanzees." *Journal of Comparative and Physiological Psychology*, 49 (1956), 223–26. (c)

347. Welker, W. I. "An Analysis of Exploration and Play Behavior in Animals." In *Functions of Varied Experience*, edited by D. W. Fiske and S. R. Maddi. Homewood, Illinois: Dorsey Press, 1961.

348. Werry, J. S. and R. L. Sprague, "Hyperactivity." In *Symptoms of Pscyhopathology*, edited by C. G. Costello. New York: John Wiley & Sons, 1970.

349. White, R. W. "Motivation Reconsidered: The Concept of Competence." *Psychological Review*, 66 (1959), 297–334.

350. Whitfield, D. "Human Skill as a Determinant of the Allocation of Function." *Ergonomics* (1967), 154–60.

351. Wiebé, E. and M. Bradley. *Quarter Century Edition of the Paradise of Childhood.* New York: Milton Bradley, 1896.

352. Wiggin, K. D. *Children's Rights. A Book of Nursery Logic.* New York: Houghton, Mifflin & Co., 1896.

353. Wiggin, K. D. and N. A. Smith. *The Republic of Childhood. III. Kindergarten Principles and Practice.* New York: Houghton, Mifflin & Co., 1896.

354. Witt, P. A. "Position Preferences in Play: A Further Study." Internal report. Motor Performance & Play Research Laboratory, Children's Research Center, University of Illinois, 1970.

355. Witt, P. A. "Dosage Effects of Methylphenidate on the Activity Level of Hyperactive Children." Unpublished PhD Dissertation. University of Illinois, 1971.

356. Witt, P. A. and A. F. Gramza. "Position Effects in Play Equipment Preferences of Nursery School Children." *Perceptual and Motor Skills*, 31 (1970), 431–34.

357. Witt, P. A. and L. H. Wuellner. Unpublished material presented and cited in L. H. Wuellner, "A Method to Investigate the Movement Patterns of Children." Unpublished Master's Thesis. University of Illinois, 1969.

358. Wohlwill, J. F. "Amount of Visual Exploration as Differential Function of Stimulus Complexity." *Perception and Psychophysics*, 4(5) (1968), 307–12.

359. Wolff, H. S. "The Integrating Motor Pneumotachograph: A New Instrument for the Measurement of Energy Expenditure by Direct Calorimetry." *Quarterly Journal of Experimental Physiology*, 43 (1958), 270–83.

360. Woodworth, R. S. *Dynamics of Behavior*. New York: Henry Holt and Co., 1958.

Wuellner, L. H. "A Method to Investigate the Movement Patterns of Children."
361. Unpublished Master's Thesis. University of Illinois, 1969.

Wuellner, L. H. "Gross Activity of Children at Play." Internal Report. Motor Performance & Play Research Laboratory, Children's Research Center, University of Illinois, 1970. (a)

362. Wuellner, L. H. "The Present Status of Research on Playgrounds." *Educational Products Information Exchange Report*, May-June 3(8–9) (1970). (b)

363. Wuellner, L. H., P. A. Witt, and R. E. Herron. "A Method to Investigate the Movement Patterns of Children." Presentation to National Recreation and Parks Association, 1970 Annual Convention, Chicago.

364. Wuellner, L. H., P. A. Witt, and R. J. Korb. "A Further Assessment of a System to Record Movement and Equipment Use Patterns." Internal Report. Motor Performance & Play Research Laboratory, Children's Research Center, University of Illinois, 1969.

365. Young, P. T. "The Role of Hedonic Processes in Motivation." In *Nebraska Symposium on Motivation, 1955*, edited by M. R. Jones. Lincoln, Nebraska: University of Nebraska Press, 1955. 193–238.

366. Young, P. T. and E. Shuford, Jr. "Intensity, Duration, and Repetition of Hedonic Processes as Related to Acquisition of Motives." *Journal of Comparative and Physiological Psychology*, 47 (1954), 298–305.

367. Zajonc, R. B. "Social Facilitation." *Science*, 149 (1965), 269–74.

368. Zajonc, R. B. "Attitudinal Effects of Mere Exposure." *Journal of Personality and Social Psychology. Monograph Supplement*, 9 (2, Pt. 2) (1968).

369. Zajonc, R. B., and D. W. Rajecki. "Exposure and Affect: A Field Experiment." *Psychonomic Science*, 17 (1969), 216–17.

370. Zajonc, R. B., P. Shaver, C. Tavris, and D. V. Kreveld. "Exposure, Satiation, and Stimulus Discriminability." *Journal of Personality and Social Psychology*, 21 (1972), 270–80.

371. Zajonc, R. B., W. C., Swap, A. A. Harrison, and P. Roberts. "Limiting Conditions of the Exposure Effect: Satiation and Relativity." *Journal of Personality and Social Psychology*, 18 (1971), 386–91.

372. Zubeck, J. P. (ed.) *Sensory Deprivation: Fifteen Years of Research*. New York: Appleton Century-Crofts, 1969.

DEPENDENT VARIABLE   ARITHMETIC DERIVATION

A!. Herron, R. E., and Frobish, M. J. "Computer Analysis and Display of Movement Patterns." *Journal of Experimental Child Psychology* 8 (1969), 40–44.

1. Each child's changes in position during each play session displayed graphically, in chronological order, on a plan view of the play area.

Arithmetic derivations for each variable were not provided.

2. The distance represented by the total changes in position of each child per play session and the mean distance for each child over all sessions.

3. The aggregate distance between each child and each of the other children for each exposure and for each play session.

4. The mean distance between each child and each of the other children for each play session computed and displayed as a function of time (i.e., with succeeding play sessions).

5. The frequency of entry of each child into each of the specified territories for each play session computed and displayed as a function of time.

6. The frequency each child is alone in each territory per play session and the incidence of solitary activity computed and displayed as a function of time.

DEPENDENT VARIABLE	ARITHMETIC DERIVATION
7. The frequency each child is accompanied by selected permutations of other children in each territory per play session computed and displayed as a function of time.	
8. The aggregate frequency of entries by all children into each of the specified territories for each play session computed and displayed as a function of time.	

AII. Wuellner, L. H. "A Method to Investigate the Movement Patterns of Children." Unpublished M. S. thesis. University of Illinois, 1969 also
  "Gross Activity of Children at Play". Presentation and mimeo. Research Section Meetings of the National Recreation and Park Association Annual Convention, Chicago, 1970.

1. Total Number of Exposures on Equipment	1. Frequency Count of each equipment item coded as used.
2. Total Number of Visits = Number of Times on Equipment over Successive Exposures	2. Frequency Count of number of changes of equipment number.
3. Average Visit Length	3. Number of exposures on Equipment (1) Divided by Number of Visits
4. Average Distance Moved (in each interval)	4. $\sum_{i=1}^{n} \dfrac{\sqrt{(X_i - X_j)^2 + (Y_i - Y_j)^2}}{n}$ where n — number of intervals (89) X — yards on X axis and Y = yards on Y axis
5. Number of Intervals Moving = Number of Times Position in One Exposure Differs from Position in Previous Exposure	5. Frequency Count
6. Velocity = Average Distance Moved When Moving (Based on Intervals in which movement occurs)	6. Total Distance (4) divided by Number of Intervals Moving (5) Min = 0

AIII. Linford *et al.* A computerized analysis of characteristics of Down's Syndrome and Normal Children's Free Play Patterns. *Journal of Leisure Research*, 3, 44–52, 1971.

1. Mean number of yards moved per frame	Same as II4
2. Average velocity in yards per frame when moving	Same as II6

DEPENDENT VARIABLE	ARITHMETIC DERIVATION
3. Percentage of frames in movement	$\dfrac{f(X_i \neq X_j \text{ and/or } Y_i \neq Y_j)}{89} \times 100$
4. Percent time spent on apparatus	$\dfrac{f(\text{on any item of apparatus})}{90} \times 100$
5. Percent time spent of each item of apparatus	$\dfrac{f(\text{on each item})}{90} \times 100$

AIV. Witt, P. A. "Dosage Effects of Methylphenidate on the Activity Level of Hyperactive Children." Unpublished Ph.D. Dissertation. University of Illinois, 1971 and Ellis, M. J., P. A. Witt, R. Reynolds, and R. L. Sprague. "Methylphenidate and the Activity of Hyperactives in the Informal Setting." Unpublished technical report. MPPRL Children's Research Center, 1972 (Experiment 2)

$$IV = \frac{\sum_{i=1}^{n-1} \left(\sqrt{(x_i - x_{i+1})^2 + (y_i - y_{i+1})^2} - \dfrac{TD}{n-1} \right)}{n-1}$$

1. Intravariance of Movement (IV). IV, or the standard deviation of four-second interval distance moved scores, was presumed to be a measure of movement style since it measured the variability of the distances moved during four-second intervals.

   where x_i and y_i = a S's coordinate position for the ith picture.
   x, y = coordinates
   $n - 1$ = number of intervals
   TD = total distance

2. Number of Intervals Moving (MI). MI equalled the number of times a S's XY position in one exposure differed from his XY position in the previous exposure. MI was included as an index of activity level.

   $MI = \sum (XY_i \neq XY_{i+1})$
   where MI = frequency of intervals moving

3. Number of Frames on Equipment (EFT).
   EFT indicated the attention paid to all pieces of equipment in the play-room during a session. It was supposed to provide an overall indication of interest level.

   $EFT = \sum_{j=1}^{m} E_j$
   where m = the number of pieces of equipment
   E_j = the frequency of use of equipment j.

4. Number of Visits to Equipment (VN).
   VN indicated the number of times a S changes from one piece of equipment or open space to another piece of equipment. Alternatively, VN can be thought of as the number of separate occurrences of equipment usage.

   $VN = \sum (E_i \neq E_{i+1})$
   where VN = frequency
   E_i = equipment visited in i^{th} frame

DEPENDENT VARIABLE	ARITHMETIC DERIVATION

5. Total Distance Moved (*TD*).
   TD indicated the total horizontal movement of a *S* over a session. It thus provided an index of gross activity level or total lateral energy expenditure.

$$TD = \sum_{i=1}^{n-1} \sqrt{(x_i - x_{i+1})^2 + (y_i - y_{i+1})^2}$$

6. Average Velocity of Movement (*VM*).
   VM measured a *S*'s average distance moved during intervals when he was moving or how fast a *S* moved when he moved. *VM* was intended as an additional index of movement style.

$$VM = TD/MI$$

7. Average Length of Visit (*VA*).
   VA reflected the attraction or average holding power of all pieces of equipment thus giving an indication of attention span.

$$VA = EFT/VN$$

8. Gross Energy Units (*GE*).
   GE equalled the percentage of intervals during a session (*N* − 1 = 149) in which a *S* *either* moved more than 1.41 yards or was on the rope net. Thus, a *S* who moved a large increment during interval one, but moved little during interval two while playing on the rope net, would have been recorded as exhibiting two units of gross energy.

$$GE = D + F$$

$$F = \frac{\sum_{j=1}^{m} E_{\text{net+trestle}}}{n}$$

$$D = \sum_{i=1}^{n-1} \frac{(\sqrt{(x_i - x_{i+1})^2 + (y_i - y_{i+1})^2})}{n-1} > 1.4$$

9. Proportion of Frames on Each Piece of Equipment (*EF_j*).
   EF_j equalled the number of frames a child was using (on or touching) the *j*th piece of equpiment during a given session divided by the total number of frames per session (150). These measures reflected the distribution of attention between the six different pieces of equipment.

$$EF_j = E_j/N$$
where *E* = number of times on the *j*th piece of equipment.

AV. Karlsson, K. A. "Hyperactivity and Environmental Compliance." Unpublished Ph.D. Dissertation. University of Illinois at Urbana, 1970.

1. Total distance moved (*TOTD*)   Same as IV5

DEPENDENT VARIABLE	ARITHMETIC DERIVATION
2. Proportion of intervals spent moving (*PRPM*)	$PRPM = \dfrac{f(XY_t \neq XY_{t+1})}{n-1}$
3. Distance moved when moving (*DMWM*)	Same as II6
4. Intravariance of movement (*INTM*)	Same as IV1
5. Total number of visits to apparatus (*VSTS*)	Same as IV4
6. Proportion of intervals on apparatus *PIAO* = intervals on floor *PIAI* = intervals on maze	$\left.\begin{array}{l}PIAO\\PIAI\end{array}\right\} = \Sigma\, E$ Where E = coded "on equipment for that frame."
7. Standard Deviation of Distance moved per interval (*SDID*)	*SD* of distance moved including intervals in which movement = 0 yards
8. Heart rate (*HTRT*)	Mean of heart rates for 20 second intervals throughout the play session for each subject.
9. Standard deviation of heart rate (*HRSD*)	Standard deviation of 20 second heart rates in each session for each subject.
10. Observation Score (*OBSV*)	Number of "observed episodes" in a play session. Episode was "a sequence (or period) of play activity unified by its logical relation to a goal inferred by two naive independent observers".

AVI. Ellis, M. J., P. A. Witt, R. Reynolds, and R. L. Sprague. "Methylphenidate and the Activity of Hyperactives in the Informal Setting". Unpublished internal report. MPPRL, Children's Research Center, 1972 (Experiment 1).

1. Intravariance of movement	Same as IV1
2. Number of intervals spent moving	Same as IV2
3. Total distance moved	Same as IV5

AVII. Gramza, A. F. "Stereotypies of Normal Children in a Boredom Setting". Abstract of project in process. Annual Report of the Motor Performance and Play Research Laboratory, 1974.

Hand fidget	Manipulate body
Facial contortion	Body sway
Body fidget	Finger mouthing
Arm fidget	Body contortion
Lean against wall	Jump

Foot fidget	Body twist
Leg fidget	Knee bend
Pace, walk	Head hold
Manipulate environs	Vocalize
Manipulate head	Manipulate crotch
Crouch, sit on floor	Crawl, roll on floor
Bounce against wall	Shoulder hunch
Manipulate clothing	Arm swing
Head fidget	Hand clapping
	Lateral body rock
	Step-trace tape square

Note: These behavioral categories are arranged in descending order of frequency
of occurrence.

AVIII. Barnett, L. A. "An Information Processing Model of Children's Play."
Unpublished M. S. Thesis. University of Illinois at Champaign, 1974. Also a
paper presented to the Second International Symposium on Play, Atlanta,
Ga. 1974.

1. Investigation (*INV*) is comprised of attempts to identify or classify the toy puzzle's
   response characteristics by *S* introducing changes in the puzzle. Involves
   physical or visual manipulation of the puzzle to discern its salient characteristics. Starts when the elements of the puzzle are tested by manipulations presumed to elicit responses from the toy puzzle. *S* attempts to
   identify a task demand and develop a strategy as a result of his investigation of the puzzle. This category finishes when *S* begins to respond to
   the inferred task demand.
2. Execution (*EXEC*) is emitting a systematic series of responses logically related to
   the realization of the inferred goal. There may be more than one execution phase in succession. They are identified separately as a series of
   responses organized to achieve different goals.
3. Investigation/Manipulation (*I/M*) is a combination of investigation and execution
   behaviors as *S* engages with task demand. Occurs as *S* begins to respond
   to the strategized goal and sequentially inspects response behaviors as
   to their efficacy in the procedural manipulatory behaviors toward realization of the goal.
4. Procedural Offtask-Clock (*OFFTPRO(C)*) includes all behaviors determined by the
   procedure where *S* is not attending to the toy puzzle. Specifically included
   are behaviors involved with the clock, such as watching or counting
   numbers and pointing.
5. Procedural Offtask-Electrodes (*OFFTPRO(E)*) involves visual exploration or
   physical manipulation of electrodes, wires, and other related apparatus.
6. Miscellaneous Offtask (*MISOFFT*) includes nonspecific explorations of the setting,
   i.e., fidgeting, looking around the room, etc., plus anything uncategori-
   zable.

7. Novel Ontask (*NOVONT*) involves novel activity related directly to the puzzle. One behavioral segment includes S generating and subsequently responding to a strategy which results in behavior other than that directed toward the initial task demand. No differentiation is made as to the components of this activity, e.g., investigation or execution.
8. Novel Offtask (*NOVOFFT*) involves a series of logically related responses directed toward anything other than the toy puzzle itself. Activity is scored *in toto* with no regard as to its component behavioral responses.
9. Old Ontask (*OLDONT*) is repetition of the initial task demand. Each successful solution of the toy puzzle marks the end of this category. There may be more than one occurrence of this category in succession; each is scored separately.

AIX. Bishop, D. W., and C. A. Chace. "Parental Conceptual Systems, Home Play Environment and Potential Creativity." *Journal of Experimental Child Psychology*, 12 (1971), 318–38.

These measures can be more easily visualized if one imagines each child having a 6 × 9 matrix of data with entries of 1 or 0 (1 if he used that figure, 0 if he did not).

1. Relative complexity of choices.
This was the sum of the number of choices of the three lowest complexity figures minus the sum for the three highest.
2. Mean number of inflection points in figures used.
This was a weighted mean obtained by multiplying the number of inflection points in a given type of shape, times the number of figures of that shape used, summing over all figures and dividing by total number of figures used.
Measures (1) and (2) are different indexes of basically the same phenomenon—the degree of complexity of the figures chosen by the child. (1) would be expected to give a sharper differentiation among Ss because it includes only the extreme selections. It was hypothesized that the children of more abstract parents would score relatively low on (1) and high on (2).
3. Relative variation in choice of color.
This measured the degree to which the child distributed his choices over all colors, at one extreme, in contrast to choosing only one color, at the other extreme. The actual measure was the standard deviation of the row marginals of the child's data matrix, divided by the mean number of figures used per row (i.e., the coefficient of variation of the row marginals).
4. Relative variation in choice of shape.
This measured the degree to which the child distributed his choices over all shapes. The measure was obtained like that in (3) by finding the coefficient of variation of column marginals.
5. Combined variation in color and shape.
This was similar to (3) and (4) but represented that portion of the total variation in a child's choices that could not be attributed to either color or shape alone. The present measure, therefore, indicated the interaction of shape and color in the child's data matrix. The actual measure was a coefficient of variation using the

square root of the interaction mean square of the child's data matrix, divided by the total mean. The assumption was that potentially creative children would use a greater variety of colors and shapes either directly or in combination. Thus, it was hypothesized that the children of more abstract parents would show *lower* scores on (3) and higher scores on (5).

6. Variation in sequence of choices.

Unlike the above measures of variation, which indicated the distribution of all the child's choices over color and shape, this measure indicated the extent to which the child varied, from one choice to the next, the column or row of the stimulus board (and therefore the shape or color) from which he made his selection. This measure was obtained by tracing an imaginary line on the child's stimulus board, connecting his choices of figures in the sequence in which he made them, and then counting the number of bends or inflection points in this line. The child who followed a systematic pattern of choices across columns or down rows of the stimulus board, regardless of his starting point in the matrix, would get a low score.

AX. Banks, M. D. "Interactive Effects of Conceptual Development of Parents and Teachers on Enhancing Creativity in Children and Conditions of Home Play." Unpublished Ph.D. Dissertation. University of Illinois, 1973.

Flexibility categories for the ball toy:
1. Bounce (B)
2. Dribble (D)
3. Kick (K)
4. On it (O)—sit, stand, roll (rolling the ball around the body)
5. Roll (R)—roll ball(s) on the floor, roll one on top of the other ball
6. Throw (T)
7. Juggle (J)

Flexibility categories for the doll toy:
1. Doll care (C)—changing the doll (wetting), bathing, combing hair
2. Feeding Doll (F)—preparing food, burping, wiping mouth
3. Holding Doll (H)—show of affection
4. Talking to Doll (T)—organized story, about going shopping, picnic, etc.
5. Putting Doll to Bed (B)
6. Going on a Trip (G)—going for a walk, for a car ride, plane ride, etc.
7. Show of Discipline (D)

Flexibility categories for the wheel toys:
1. Delivery (L)—loading—appliances, animals, building material, food, furniture, toys
2. Unloading (U)—any unloading procedure
3. Operating Truck (O)—Moving truck forward or backward, making truck sounds
4. Repair (R)—changing flat, fix engine, fix broken glass, etc.
5. Service Station Stop (S)—getting gasoline, oil, windows washed
6. Wash and Clean (W)
7. Wreck (X)

Flexibility categories for the complex block toy:
1. Alphabets or numbers
2. Architectural Structures—towers, wall, tunnel, arch, bridge
3. Animals
4. Buildings—house, factory, garage
5. Design—name or function puzzle, statue
6. Furniture—chair, table, bed, bench
7. Transportation—airplane, car, bus, truck, submarine, boat

The subject's play behavior was recorded on a work sheet designed for this experiment. The experimenter used a number to identify each category and letter to abbreviate responses in each category, and then wrote out a brief description of the activity. An example of one such item on the play behavior test is:

Ball toy: 1 B-2 + caught
Interpretation: A ball toy was being used by the subject.
He let the ball bounce twice on the floor and caught it.

—This was used to indicate that there was a change in category.

The specific measures which were obtained from the Banks Play Behavior Test are as follows:

Fluency—total number of acceptable responses. An acceptable response is any response which the subject gives while playing with toy(s), and is not a duplicate or repeat of an earlier response.

Flexibility—The flexibility score was obtained by counting the number of different categories in which the responses fall. Listed below are the toys and categories that were used to fit the responses of the subjects. Any new categories generated during the play session were listed below and other categories as "X1" for the first new category, "X2" for the second new category, etc. . . A category could be counted more than once, e.g., as long as the subject had given a response from a different category.

Uniqueness—(originality)—number of responses given by only one child in the sample. These responses were taken from the fluency responses. The subject scored a unique response if he and only he gave a response that no other person in the experiment gave.

Rate—the number of responses produced in a given time interval. The rate of responses was determined by counting the total number of acceptable responses given during each one minute time interval.

AXI. Reynolds, R. P., and M. J. Ellis. "The Operant Training of Creativity in Children." Mimeo, 1974.

The following measures of creativity were obtained from the video tape recordings of treatment sessions. The first three verbal content categories were derived from the classification of Torrance (1966). The remaining variables were derived for this study.
1. Fluency—Total number of acceptable responses. An acceptable response was any verbal label which the subject gave upon completing an item constructed which was not a duplicate of an earlier label.

2. Flexibility—This score was obtained by counting the number of different categories into which the responses of each child fell.
3. Unique Responses—A unique response was defined as a response no other child had given.
4. Total number of responses.—This score was obtained by summing the total number of verbal labels given by a child.
5. Total number of blocks used in construction—Obtained by counting the number of blocks in each of the final constructions and summing these totals.

AXII. Scholtz, G. J. L. "Environmental Novelty and Complexity as Determinants of Children's Play." Unpublished PhD Dissertation. University of Illinois, 1973.

Object Preference or Apparatus Interaction. Engagement with the apparatus setting was computed by summing all frames for all children in overt contact with the play apparatus.	Same as IV3.
Peer Preference or Group play in the open space. The variable was scored using an anecdotal record of activity, together with inferences about sequences of frames. Peer preference occurred when a child overtly interacted with one or more peers in the space away from the play apparatus.	Frequency count for each child, summed over children for each session.

Appendix B/ **Camera Details**

Nikon F camera, with model F250 accessory (250 exposure motor drive body).
Accura fish-eye lens fitted to 50 mm f 1.4 *Nikor* lens resulting in combined focal length of 7.5 mm and an angle of acceptance of 180°.
Film Tri-X 35 mm, processed at Exposure Index of 1000 and printed in a Bell and Howell M and J movie printer on fine grain release positive film.
Both negative and positive were processed in a Kodak Versamat.
Exposure 1/125 sec. at f 5.6.

Appendix **C | Description**

# of Heart Rate Telemeter

1. The design of the transmitter unit was divided into three parts: first, an oscillator which supplied the antenna with the modulated FM signal transmitted to an FM receiver located outside the playroom laboratory; second, an antenna suitable for transmitting the HR information through space with minimal body effects and without trauma to the subjects; and third, an amplifier to increase the gain of the 1 mv signal to an amplitude sufficient to modulate the oscillator. The input signal was picked up by electrodes. Electrodes were manufactured by Biosensory Products, International Biophysics Corp., 2700 DuPont Drive, Irvine, California 92664, were placed on the subject's skin and applied to the input of the amplifier. The system's requirements specified that the oscillator had to be small, operate on a low voltage, and transmit approximately 50 yd. A standard FM receiver was already used in the system; therefore, the oscillator had to be designed to operate in the FM band. A Colpitts oscillator was chosen because it met most of the initial requirements; it was then modified. A capacitor voltage divided network was added to the oscillator to help isolate the antenna from the oscillator tank circuit in order to reduce frequency shifting produced by body effects. The base-to-emitter bias resistor was replaced by a capacitor, so the FM oscillator could be modulated by the heart beat once it was amplified. The rest of the values for the oscillator were taken from a circuit already tested and working.

2. For continuous recording of the heart rate, an antenna that would radiate in a 360° pattern was needed. This proved a difficult requirement to fulfill since the subjects were involved in activities that represented almost all positions with respect to the receiving antenna. Another important factor was that the subject's body shielded part of the radiating area, because the transmitter was mounted at the waist. A monopole type antenna fitted most of the requirements and several test trials were conducted using various configurations, lengths, and materials. Tests showed a rigidly mounted banana plug to be satisfactory for most of the requirements placed on the antenna. Two advantages in using a banana plug

were that a plastic cap shielded the metal part of the plug, and the plug was short enough not to harm the subject.

3. The amplifier required (a) input impedance of approximately 10 K-ohms, (b) enough amplification of the 1 mv signal to modulate the oscillator, (c) a stability factor of approximately 10, and (d) low operating voltage. The transistor chosen (2N3707) met the basic requirements and was used to design two stages of amplification. A diagram of the circuit is shown in Figure 1.

The circuit was to be mounted in as small an area as possible, which presented a problem because the unit had to contain a switch, input leads, a battery, and the antenna. The amplifier and oscillator were mounted in a close knit fashion. A small copper box was then constructed to contain the transmitter component. The box was designed to be mounted on the child's belt by a clip. The copper box was used to isolate the circuit components from as many body effects as possible. The circuit was then potted in a silicone compound to reduce any effect caused by strong shocks received during play. In order to facilitate the removal of the input leads, pin jacks, mounted on the copper box, were used.

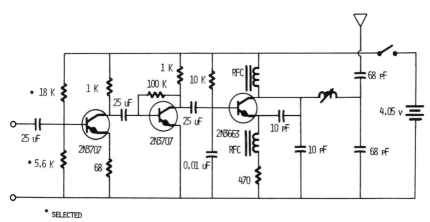

Fig. C.1:   Schematic for the heart rate telemeter.

Compared to the Portable Helmet

DOUGLAS VALVE (limitations)	HELMET
1. Rubber mouth-piece required	1. No mouth-piece required
a. Forces subject to breath through the mouth	a. Breathing is normal.
b. Creates a consciousness of breathing	b. Subject's consciousness of breathing is not affected
c. Biting down on the mouth piece holds the valve in place	c. Helmet is held in place by head and shoulder supports
d. Often causes drying of the mouth (cotton mouth)	d. No drying of the mouth when using the helmet
e. Swallowing is difficult while breathing through the mouth and biting mouth piece.	e. No difficulty swallowing
2. Valve required.	2. No valve required.
a. 55 ml. of dead air space	a. No dead air space
b. 54 mm. of water at 150 liters per minute resistance to steady flow	b. No resistance to steady flow
c. Minor leaks significantly affect the results	c. Minor leaks have no effect on results
3. Additional equipment required	3. No additional equipment required
a. Tubing from valve to measuring equipment and sampling equipment	a. No tubing required
b. Sampling equipment needed	b. Sampling is a function of the helmet
c. Volume measuring equipment needed	c. Volume of sample is repre sentative of total volume
4. Movement is restricted by hoses and other equipment	4. Movement is not restricted

Courtesy L. E. Foster

Appendix E | Portable Respiratory Helmet Construction

The following is a discussion of the individual components of the helmet as they are proposed.

Air Inlets: The helmet had three air inlets. There will be one inlet on each side and one on the top. Each inlet will be connected to a coil of tygon tubing to prevent leakage. The air flow is directed to create a circulating and cooling effect. After the air is expired by the subject, it will be drawn through two plastic canals with the other air and then pass through the squirrel cage fan of the motor unit.

Shell: The shell was an Apollo program space bubble donated by NASA. The bubble has a nine inch opening for the head to pass through. The head, after being placed in the helmet is located in a hollow ellipsoid with a $12\frac{1}{2}$-inch longitudinal diameter and a 9-inch transverse diameter. The bubble was shatterproof transparent polycarbonate.

Support of the Helmet: The helmet was supported by a head band similar to those used with head phones. These head bands adjust automatically to nearly all head sizes. With the use of the head band the helmet will move and turn with the head. There will be additional support at the shoulders with a plastic-covered, foam rubber disc which will also prevent a leak at the neck. The plastic-covered, foam disc will be attached to the helmet by use of a cable and spring around the circumference of the opening for the head.

Vacuum Motor: The motor is a "Miniature Commutatorless D. C. Centrifugal Blower," model TB-2.5, built by the Brailsford & Company, Inc. The motor operates at the efficiency of D. C. motor while attaining the long life and quiet running characteristics of an A. C. device. The electro-dynamic efficiency of the complete unit reaches slightly over 60% and delivers approximately 18 cubic feet of free air per minute on a power drain of 2.16 watts. The motor will be run at a voltage of 24 volts with a power input of 1.0 amperes. The motor will operate at 3200 R.P.M. The weight of the unit is 14 ounces. The motor is designed so as not to interfere with radio transmission.

Listed below are descriptive terms of behavior. Place a check mark in the column which best describes this child. ANSWER ALL ITEMS. In filling out this checklist consider only the past 4 weeks.

OBSERVATION	DEGREE OF ACTIVITY			
	Not at All	*Just a Little*	*Pretty Much*	*Very Much*
(18) Constantly fidgeting				
(19) Hums and makes other odd noises				
(20) Restless or overactive				
(21) Excitable, impulsive				
(22) Disturbs other children				
(23) Teases other children or interferes with their activities				
(24) Excessive demands for teacher's attention				
(25) Overly anxious to please				

Please add any information of particular note concerning this child's attitude towards class activities and his behavior within the classroom.

Subject Index

Author Index